Th

Rog
Arti
at Q
are

Penguin Masterstudies
Joint Advisory Editors:
Stephen Coote and Bryan Loughrey

Henry James

The Portrait of a Lady

Roger Gard

Penguin Books

...in Books Ltd, Harmondsworth, Middlesex, England
Viking Penguin Inc., 40 West 23rd Street, New York, New York 10010, U.S.A.
Penguin Books Australia Ltd, Ringwood, Victoria, Australia
Penguin Books Canada Limited, 2801 John Street, Markham, Ontario, Canada L3R 1B4
Penguin Books (N.Z.) Ltd, 182–190 Wairau Road, Auckland 10, New Zealand

First published 1986

Copyright © Roger Gard, 1986
All rights reserved

Made and printed in Great Britain by
Richard Clay (The Chaucer Press) Ltd, Bungay, Suffolk
Filmset in Monophoto Times

Contents

Note to the Reader and Acknowledgements

A knowledge of the novel is assumed throughout. A knowledge of other of James's works would be extremely useful – extremely.

Maisie Gard, Simon and Beryl Gray, and Kit Price have been very helpful in various ways.

The text referred to is that published by Penguin Books (see Appendix). Page numbers refer to this text. For those reading other editions, chapter numbers are given.

I Introduction

1. Formidable James

The Portrait of a Lady, published in 1881, when he was 38, was Henry James's first long masterpiece, both the culmination and climax of his early work – a fact of which he was constantly aware while writing it: 'I must try and seek a larger success than I have yet obtained in doing something on a larger scale than I have yet done,' he wrote to his friend W. D. Howells in 1879, and such remarks are scattered through his letters of the period.

Readers will have noticed that the book is indeed on a large scale: and so it is important to suggest immediately a modification to the general and daunting view of James as merely extremely hard work for the reader, and therefore another case of what Martin Dodsworth with appropriate distaste calls:

... the host of introductions, guides and casebooks, which imply a gap between the reader's interest and aptitude and what the books introduced ... have to say, a gap that has to be bridged by the indefatigable introducers. (*New Pelican Guide to English Literature*, Vol. 8, p. 491).

This introducer hopes to be intensely fatigable, though not fatiguing, and must insist from the start that while *The Portrait of a Lady* is a classic it is not therefore boring and inaccessible, but brilliantly witty, compelling, and moving, as well as subtle and profound. For anyone who likes literature at all, it is a novel to be read for pleasure and excitement; not a 'text' to be plodded doggedly through. This becomes obvious after a couple of chapters to most readers. And they will be sceptical of the arcane reflections – praise as fulsome and turgid as it is commonly inaccurate – of some of his admirers who, proud of *their* mastery of the difficult later novels, expatiate off-puttingly on James's status as the 'Master' (a Continental term which unfortunately in his later loneliness he did not dislike) and thus frighten us off or convince us, wrongly, that he became an exquisite overpowering *windbag*. In fact, James offers far more straight pleasures than obscure pains.

2. Life

Henry James's life was both uneventful and complex. Unlike some great artists he was compelled neither by financial nor external necessity to lead other than an intensely private existence. He never seriously had to earn money, nor was he led by conviction or circumstance to play a role in public – as were, to take random examples, Milton, Fielding, Byron, Shelley, Dickens or Ezra Pound. Even his private life was more than usually private since he never married and, in spite of his warmth to a galaxy of male and female friends, does not seem to have had really intimate relationships with anyone. There are hints that he much appreciated late in life the admiration of a number of handsome young men: but hints are all that these are and it would be futile as well as prurient to consider his 'sex-life' further. This does not, I think, make him uninteresting as a man: but it does mean that it is only necessary to burden the reader with a brief sketch of his career. A procedure of which he would have approved.

James was born in New York in 1843. His grandfather, William James, had emigrated poor from Ireland to become one of the great financial successes and pillars of the community of his period. He was a rigid Presbyterian and left about $3,000,000, then an *immense* sum, to be divided between his eleven children. The Jameses were, therefore, part of America's new élite, resident in Albany, the capital of New York State; a new élite not just in riches and influence but, as it turned out, in extraordinary talents. James's father (Henry James Sr) was, as well as a man of leisure, a thinker, a theologian, and a follower of the Swedish mystic Swedenborg. His thoughts led his children into an eccentric educational dance which nevertheless produced a vastly influential (and still influential) psychologist and philosopher, William James, as well as his younger brother, the novelist. This education, under a variety of systems, veered between America and Europe until 1860 when, settling in America Henry James Jr suffered an 'obscure' physical hurt which prevented him from taking part in the major traumatic event of his generation, the American Civil War. After an unsympathetic brush with the Law School at Harvard he began seriously, deliberately, with implacable purpose, but slowly, to embrace his career as a writer. In 1870 his young cousin, Minny Temple, died of tuberculosis, and the hurt was, this time, not totally obscure: James wrote of her to his mother as the 'very heroine of our common scene', of 'how much I knew her and how much I loved her', of 'that wonderful ethereal brightness of presence that was so peculiarly her own', and 'Twenty years hence what a pure eloquent vision she will be'. As this last phrase suggests, it is not certain that James was, in our ordinary sense, 'in love' with his cousin. But it is reasonable to argue (as many critics do) that her memory became his central source for the pure and innocent and radiant American girl of many of his fictions, most notably *The Portrait of a Lady* and *The Wings of the Dove* (1902).

After publishing his first (rather poor) novel *Watch and Ward* in 1871, James lived briefly in Paris in 1875 where, as in America, he became acquainted with many of the literary and intellectual forces of his time. In 1876, having 'seen round' the French, he established himself in London. There, although always travelling abroad, he settled until 1897, when he bought a house in Rye. He revisited America in 1882 (twice) on the deaths of his parents; and in 1904–5 when he saw cause to revise drastically downwards his estimate of that burgeoning capitalist culture. In 1915 he became a British citizen in protest at America's delayed entry into the First World War. In 1916 he died having received – possibly without knowing it – the Order of Merit. A Grand Old Man, the subject of a cult, but little read by the general public which he had hoped, in vain, to find.

Such a summary gives an extremely misleading impression of an artist living in an ivory tower (the ironic title, incidentally, of one of his last unfinished novels). James was a deeply professional writer. I have no space to list his prolific output – at least forty-four volumes of novels and short fictions, literary criticism, art criticism, travel writing, plays, reviews, biography and autobiography, etc. Such a list is easily available elsewhere. While having no absolute need for financial success, he acutely bargained for it, and missed it. His attempt to capture acclaim in the theatre (c. 1890–5 and at other times) was also, and predominantly, his major albeit not only attempt to reach a wider audience, to be appreciated outside 'artistic circles'. It was a humiliating failure. But the author as seen through letters, reminiscences and biographies was a handsome man, a great diner-out, intensely social, brilliantly witty, of immense charm and formidable intellect. He always moved in the 'best' circles, socially and intellectually, although he was one of the most serious and funny critics of this environment. He predicted – and feared – social revolution and disaster in the 1880s, largely because of his horror at the state of the London slums. He pierced, and would have shamed had it read him, the decadence of 'Edwardian' society. The pertinence, even savagery, of his accounts, with their deceptively benign tone, only began to be widely realized twenty or thirty years after his death. Now, of course, he is a classic, a paperback author, and a set text.

Part of James's peculiar quality (which he shares with Conrad) is that he was a cosmopolitan. Is he an English novelist? an American novelist? or something else altogether? – it is a subject of extensive debate. Whether this (whichever you settle for) is an advantage or the reverse is equally debatable, equally not to be settled. But the remarks of T. S. Eliot, another patrician American expatriate, are suggestive:

> Some day I want to write an essay about the point of view of an American who wasn't an American . . . and who . . . felt himself to be more of a Frenchman than an American and yet felt that the U.S.A. up to a hundred years ago was a family extension. It is almost too difficult for H[enry] J[ames], who for that matter wasn't an American at all, in that sense.

Eliot never wrote that essay, but I trust that the reader will share a sense of creative confusion.

This confusion is all the more interesting nowadays because of the prominence in James's work of the 'international theme' – a tired phrase meaning that he often wrote about the interaction, or collision, of the new innocent American culture with the old corrupt, yet seductive, Europe. That Europe is often represented by expatriate Americans like James himself – as in *Portrait* – is interesting but does not, in this context, matter. After the Second World War, this seemed to most readers a useful artistic device but little more: in its context rather quaint like writing about the Wars of the Roses or the French Revolution, but essentially irrelevant. But now, I think, it has regained an odd prophetic relevance – but one which has been *turned upside down*. The United States is now seen as culturally dominant and 'corrupt', its European (or, at least, English) visitors as innocents. James's equivocal, floating, position therefore allowed him insights we can use again, but in reverse. He is willy-nilly more of a political writer than he probably would have thought. Because he was 'one of those on whom nothing is lost', *Portrait*, so apparently 'dated' and 'delightful' has more to say about this admittedly peripheral realm than might at first appear.

Finally, there is a wealth of anecdote about James. But the truest note seems to me to be struck by his then young friend, Ford Madox Ford, a novelist of some genius himself, reminiscing:

> I will not say that loveableness was the predominating feature of the Old Man: he was too intent upon his own particular aims to be lavishly sentimental over surrounding humanity. And his was not a character to be painted in the flat, in water colour . . . he loved to appear in the character of a sort of Mr Pickwick – with the rather superficial benevolences, and the mannerisms of which he was perfectly aware. But below that protective mask was undoubtedly a plane of nervous cruelty. I have heard him be – to simple and quite unpretentious people –

more diabolically blighting than was quite decent for a man to be – for he was always an artist in expression. And it needed a certain fortitude when . . . his dark eyes rolled in their whites and he spoke very brutal and direct English . . . And yet there was a third depth – a depth of religious, of mystical, benevolence . . . His practical benevolences were innumerable, astonishing – and indefatigable . . . I may as well now confess that in drawing Henry VIII in my own novels I was rendering the Master in externals . . . (*Thus to Revisit: Some Reminiscences*, London, 1921).

This may be as fanciful as it is certainly melodramatic – and it *is* about the older man. But it rightly helps us to dispel the idea of James as a wistful, prolix aesthete. That Ford's verdict can be confirmed in reading *Portrait* we shall see.

3. The Literary Context

It is, of course, impossible here to even begin to give an account of the complex and volatile artistic and intellectual situation from which James wrote. So I will offer some lame generalities instead. It is a commonplace to say that the century from c. 1810 to c. 1910 saw the great flowering of two *relatively* new art forms: the Novel and the Opera. James had little taste for the latter (although he does obliquely allude to it in his work) and he even, infuriatingly, lightly declined an introduction to the great Richard Wagner. But he was, of course, very much aware of his predecessors and contemporaries in prose fiction. He inherited – unlike, for example, Jane Austen – an extremely rich range of models, experiments, successes and failures on which to build and evolve his own work. A short selection of names will enforce the point: Janes Austen herself, Stendhal, Balzac, Thackeray, Dickens, Turgenev, Hawthorne, Melville, Tolstoy, the Brontë sisters, Flaubert, George Eliot, Bourget, Daudet – the student will extend this list with ease. Even the poet Browning (on whom James wrote a fine essay) may have had some influence through his 'dramatic' verse.

Literary indebtedness is hard to establish, in spite of all the talk about it, and we will encounter it in more detail in discussing *Portrait*. But in general terms a few particularly striking, and varied, 'influences' can be indicated here: Hawthorne (in the very early work), Jane Austen (especially in *The Europeans*, 1878, and *Washington Square*, 1880), Balzac (in *Washington Square* and perhaps the 'social' novels of the 1880s), Flaubert (in the intensive artistic organization of material at first sight mundane – 'anything becomes interesting if you look at it hard enough'), Turgenev (as we shall see), Dickens (all over the place), and most importantly,

George Eliot (as we shall see also). An interesting addition to these obvious cases is Trollope on whom, Q. D. Leavis has recently argued in a posthumous essay, James relied heavily in his presentation of English life and speech (*Collected Essays*, ed. G. Singh, Vol. 2, Cambridge, 1985).

But James was of course not solely touched by other works of art or, for that matter, his intensely sociable life. Many of the tendencies of his thought and sensibility – the organs through which he perceived his world and created from it – must have been determined by the intellectual ebb and flow of his time. It has been argued with conviction by Stephen Donadio (*Nietzsche, Henry James and the Artistic Will*, O.U.P., New York, 1978) that the great German philosopher had much in common with him – indirect, but mediated through his brother William. More certainly, he must have been influenced by his father's friend, Emerson (whom he very much liked) and the peculiarly American response to the disturbance caused by a general retreat from a traditional, comfortable Christian belief called 'Transcendentalism'. The complex and reverberant issues raised by this cannot be discussed here, nor am I competent to discuss them. But the type of relevance to James of an inherited and highly critical moral sense bereft by scientists and philosophers of supernatural sanction (and frequently noted by commentators) is perhaps most provocatively expressed for our limited purpose by a remark of Donadio's on:

... the striving to break out of the net of human relations and to experience an existence unmediated by social forms (one's own reality *an sich*) – a striving reflected, for example, in Isabel Archer's attempt to define herself without relation to anyone or anything – is clearly the expression of an idea with the profoundest social and political implications ... (p. 10).

Such a remark firmly adverts us to the question of what a soul, a mind or even a personality essentially *is* where it lacks a theological background. Those especially interested in this and related questions would enjoy the classic and trenchant essay by Yvor Winters, 'Maule's Well, or Henry James and the Relation of Morals to Manners', in his *Maule's Well* (1938), reprinted in *In Defence of Reason*, London, 1960. But readers of 'mere novels' could well delay such matters until they have enjoyed *this* novel.

4. Conscious Limitation

Perhaps the most frequent objection to James's art is that he deals, on the whole, with a very limited set of people, people who have no or few obligations to the ordinary workaday world. This is not literally true, for among his major protagonists there are civil servants, a diplomat, governesses, tutors, a bookbinder, a post-office worker, a bookseller, clergymen, doctors, journalists, politicians, very many artists both plastic and literary, and very many businessmen. But it is essentially accurate in that these various occupations are kept firmly in the background with very few exceptions (the governess in *The Turn of the Screw*, for example). Thus in *Portrait* Daniel Touchett is a banker, Caspar Goodwood a master of cotton mills, Lord Warburton a prominent politician and county magnate: but we learn nothing at all about banking, cotton manufacture or politics. There are other novelists like James (Laclos, Goethe and Jane Austen spring to mind), but few so rigorously exclusive in their selection of material. This is especially striking in view of the wide range of occupation and class treated amply by those European writers who may be supposed to have influenced him – George Eliot, Dickens, Balzac and Flaubert, for instance.

Taking the objection further it can be remarked that even given his chosen material James further limits it by excluding the mundane activities of his characters. Dressing, eating, bathing, travelling, paying bills, shopping and so on receive only the most perfunctory mention. Even the painful physical facts of Ralph Touchett's tuberculosis are kept to a minimum. And this in the age of 'Naturalism' when Zola and his followers, French and English, set out to describe (in often tedious detail) the exact facts about nearly every facet of life.

The Penguin edition of *Portrait* has a note on the following passage about Ralph's joking manner:

'I keep a band of music in my ante-room', he said once to her. 'It has orders to play without stopping ... It keeps the sounds of the world from reaching the private apartments, and it makes the world think that dancing's going on within' ... Isabel ... would have liked to pass through the ante-room, as her cousin called it, and enter the private apartments. It mattered little that he had assured her they were a very dismal place; she would have been glad to undertake to sweep them and set them in order. (Ch. VII, p. 113)

The note serves usefully to jar us into fresh awareness of James's deliberate abstraction from everyday activity: '*Band of music* ... This would presumably be a music-box, or a roll from a mechanical piano.' Apart from these not being a band, it is impossible to imagine perpetual honky-tonk at Gardencourt, or even more so Isabel as a housemaid. The annotator has perhaps taken a vow to deny the existence of metaphor, or, more likely is offering some sort of joke.

At any rate there are two points to be made on this aspect of James. The first is of the take it or leave it kind: he evidently found much naturalistic detail so obvious, already known, or irrelevant, that it would have been a waste of time to write about it. The second is the positive corollary of this: his passionate interest was in presenting the subtle and violent working of the mind and spirit and moral sense – the essentials in human nature – so that he had to rid his fiction of much, not all, ordinary external action to achieve a precise and intense focus. I think he was both brave and justified by results.

But enough of generalities. These issues and others force themselves on our attention frequently and specifically in the detailed analysis of *Portrait* to which I shall now proceed.

II Before Marriage

1. Poor Isabel

The ancient Greek philosopher Aristotle is supposed to have said that works of art should have a beginning, a middle and an end. The banality of this observation may have been the natural result of the fact that his *Poetics* are derived only from (roughly) notes of a student listening to lectures. Nevertheless, the obvious is rarely untrue: in this case, it is still enormously influential.

Any reader will have noticed that *The Portrait of a Lady* has a very extended opening; an interesting middle; and an accelerated end. Where better to start than, in a spirit of English compromise, in the middle: with the celebrated Chapter XLII in which Isabel Archer/Osmond reflects on the consequences of her choice of life? James himself in his 1908 Preface thought that this was 'obviously the best thing in the book', and although it is possible to disagree with that judgement, it is impossible to fail to see that these meditations are an intended crux, extending back to the start of the novel and forward to its end. The reader naturally will sympathize with our heroine's plight after two years of stultifying marriage:

It was not her fault – she had practised no deception; she had only admired and believed. She had taken all the first steps in the purest confidence, and then she had suddenly found the infinite vista of a multiplied life to be a dark, narrow alley with a dead wall at the end. Instead of leading to the high places of happiness, from which the world would seem to lie below one, so that one could look down with a sense of exaltation and advantage, and judge and choose and pity, it led rather downward and earthward, into realms of restriction and depression where the sound of other lives, easier and freer, was heard as from above, and where it served to deepen the feeling of failure. (p. 474)

The reaction here, as elsewhere in this complicated chapter, will first be 'poor Isabel'. But the reader will, after a second's thought ask: who is speaking? The answer is that it is not the author but the character. And what, although we are her loyal supporters, are we to make of her account? Is Osmond a pure villain (see Section above) and is Isabel simply the injured party? At times we seem to be in no doubt:

Her notion of the aristocratic life was simply the union of great knowledge with great liberty; the knowledge would give one a sense of duty and the liberty a sense of enjoyment. But for Osmond it was altogether a thing of forms, a conscious, calculated attitude. (p. 480)

At other times Isabel questions her own actions. But the point for the reader to note is that these apparently clear vindications of Isabel by herself and for herself carry their own internal judgements. There are indications that she – by means of her most positive and candid interior monologue – betrays herself to us. The reaction of the intelligent reader has to be a question: what has she, persecuted, beset, and sympathetic as she is, envisaged as desirable? The clues are all in the prose. Never mind, for the moment, the suffering she has undergone: James is reminding us of the cause of that suffering and showing, with great precision, that it is not wholly external.

The bewildered Isabel ruminates on what she had desired, against the advice of her friends (she does not yet know how much at the *expense* of her friends), in marrying Osmond. She desired 'the high places of happiness, from which the world would seem to be below one, so that one could look down with a sense of exaltation and advantage, and judge and choose and pity'. I suppose that most people have felt such an envisaged, King of the Castle position as desirable for themselves. We have only to be frank with our daydreams. But one does not have to be an entrenched egalitarian to feel that the attitude is repulsive. Looking down with a sense of exaltation and advantage, judging and choosing, are certainly not what we want the people in our world to do to us (rather we may indulgently imagine doing it to them, which is precisely the delusive charm). But even more irritating is Isabel's vagueness: is the exaltation moral? the advantage only financial? who or what is to be judged and chosen? – and so on. The very fact that we cannot answer these questions directly and certainly oddly brings us back into sympathy with her. The superiority of an American banker, an English lord, an American *entrepreneur*, is definite and specifiable: money, power, and energy deployed for a purpose. But Isabel lives in the realm of the rosy abstract. Nevertheless she continues in her misery to try, at least, to specify her 'notion' (interesting word) of the 'aristocratic': great knowledge and liberty equal, it appears, the gift of enjoyable duty. It would perhaps be hitting her too hard to ask again what exactly these terms mean. But by now the point is taken: even in her most introspective moments, Isabel is not at all sure of herself or of her meaning. Chapter XLII is revealing, but what it mainly shows is a kind of conscientious confusion. For the source of this we have to look back in the novel: for its possible resolution forward, as I have said. We have an excellent middle. So now it is appropriate to look at the beginning.

2. An Imagined Figure

How does James want us to take his heroine at first? His brilliant account, in the Preface, of Turgenev's sympathetic creative procedure provides an illuminating comment (James's Prefaces are not always so much to the point):

I have always fondly remembered a remark that I heard fall years ago from the lips of Ivan Turgenieff in regard to his own experience of the usual origin of the fictive picture. It began for him almost always with the vision of some person or persons, who hovered before him, soliciting him, as the active or passive figure, interesting and appealing to him just as they were and by what they were. He saw them ... subject to the chances, the complications of existence, and saw them vividly, but then had to find for them the right relations, those that would most bring them out; to imagine, to invent and select and piece together the situations most useful and favourable to the sense of the creatures themselves, the complications they would be most likely to produce and feel.

'To arrive at these things is to arrive at my "story",' he said, 'and that's the way I look for it.' (p. 43)

This, continues James, sanctioned and encouraged his own instinctive methods – 'the blest habit of one's own imagination' – for 'I was myself so much more antecedently conscious of my fingers than of their setting . . .' It is a little sarcastically contrasted with writers who have a preconceived plan or purpose – a 'writer so constituted as to see his fable first and to make out his agents afterwards'. If we tease out the meaning of this, and realize that its precision is achieved by a hovering suggestion rather than by a pseudo-scientific use of 'technical' terms, we can arrive at a simple but deep truth on the lines of: Shakespeare did not set out to write a play *illustrating* the features and disasters of bloody tyranny; instead he saw before him the suffering and consequently vicious figure of Macbeth: or, on the contrary, Milton did set out to tell the divine truth about the universe in *Paradise Lost* but ended up by creating, in spite of himself, a colossal tragic hero who is the Prince of Evil.

So, how do we see Isabel at the beginning? Her main characteristic is an energetic directness. Into the relaxed, gorgeous serenity of Gardencourt and the playful light witty talk of Mr Touchett, Ralph Touchett, and Lord Warburton – a scene characterized by a plethora of adjectives: 'simple . . . admirable . . . innocent . . . perfect . . . splendid . . . finest . . .

rarest . . .' (a selection from the first page) – is suddenly introduced by the barking of a pet dog a nicely incongruent figure: 'a tall girl in a black dress, who at first sight looked pretty. She was bare-headed.' 'Dear me, who's that strange woman?' asks Mr Touchett. And we should perhaps now realize that the answer to his question is what is to be worked out in the book. Isabel has become the subject. What the reader wants to know is what she is like.

What she is like is determined by two things: the reaction of others to her and her own speech. She is envisaged, now and later, as impinging upon a rich and complicated civilization – part of the charm of which for the candid modern reader at least must lie in a sense of nostalgia for the opulence and calm of late Victorian wealth and leisure (characteristics much exploited nowadays by television, etc., and undeniably attractive in their way). The attentive reader will have noted that these gracious appearances have, even at the very beginning, not gone entirely unquestioned. Mr Touchett is curiously insistent in his doubts: 'When I was twenty years old . . . I was working tooth and nail. You wouldn't be bored if you had something to do; but all you young men are too idle. You think too much of your pleasure. You're too fastidious, and too indolent, and too rich' – and 'I'm convinced there will be great changes; and not all for the better' (pp. 64–5). Nevertheless Isabel does present a clear contrast to her setting by her immediate exhibition of a fresh New World directness: 'I've never seen anything so lovely as this place. I've been all over the house; it's too enchanting' (p. 70): or (of Mr Touchett's illness) '"Ah, poor man, I'm very sorry!" the girl exclaimed, immediately moving forward' (p. 71): or (to Mr Touchett's compliment) '"Oh, yes, of course I'm lovely!" she returned with a quick laugh. "How old is your house? Is it Elizabethan?"' (p. 72) And so on. The important summation of these remarks in Chapter II is her assertion, 'with a certain visible eagerness of desire to be explicit' that 'I'm very fond of my liberty' (p.74). The reader now has a definite sense of the 'figure' which appeared to James as repaying treatment; his other characters seem to agree. 'You wished a while ago to see my idea of an interesting woman,' says Lord Warburton, 'There it is!'

This claim of Isabel's to liberty is, of course, a key factor in the novel pursued in its many forms with great force and persistence. It brings her to the situation analysed in Chapter XLII, and from there on in a violently modified and twisted form to the end of the book. We should reflect that the pursuit of such freedom by a *single* young woman was a very different, and very much more difficult, enterprise then than it is now. Such facts are relevant to fiction. Henrietta will soon appear. But immediately, as is usual in dramatic fiction, comparison and contrast begin in a lesser form. Isabel's patroness, Mrs Touchett, who has freed her from the relative seclusion of Albany, is notably independent herself. She has her own establishment and lives her own life – an arrangement which her husband (who later sees in Isabel a potential similarity) regrets and which she herself comes at the end drily to question. Almost at once the matter is canvassed between them. Isabel would like to go to Florence:

'Well, if you'll be very good and do everything I tell you, I'll take you there,' Mrs Touchett declared.

Our young woman's emotion deepened; she flushed a little and smiled at her aunt in silence. 'Do everything you tell me? I don't think I can promise that.'

'No, you don't look like a person of that sort. You're fond of your own way; but it's not for me to blame you.' (Ch. III, p. 82)

So the 'free greyhound' is ready to set out on her career with 'her desire to leave the past behind her ... to begin afresh'. And immediately we are introduced to a related aspect of this desire: Isabel's avid and idealizing imagination.

Imagination is a key word in this book – perhaps the most important of a range of artfully reiterated concepts. And, like many words, it can afford to accommodate different emphases. In everyday life, we habitually use two almost contrary senses: 'he has no imagination' (that is, no breadth or grasp of mind); 'Oh, that's just your imagination' (that is, fancifulness and no grasp of mind). There are many shades in between. James exploits them very subtly. Immediately after Mrs Touchett's visit to Albany we are told that Isabel's:

... imagination was by habit ridiculously active; when the door was not open it jumped out of the window. She was not accustomed indeed to keep it behind bolts; and at important moments, when she would have been thankful to make use of her judgement alone, she paid the penalty of having given undue encouragement to the faculty of seeing without judging. (Ch. IV, p. 86)

This is a generalized comment, tempered by Isabel's respect for 'judgement'. But it serves as a gentle warning. A much more important and expansive commentary, a complex pre-Portrait, is strategically placed at the beginning of Chapter VI, which starts with the statement that 'Isabel Archer was a young person of many theories; her imagination was remarkably active.' We are then told of her fineness of mind, but also of the conceit, impatience and inexperience that go with it:

She had no talent for expression and too little of the consciousness of genius;

she only had a general idea that people were right when they treated her as if she were rather superior. Whether or no she were superior, people were right in admiring her if they thought her so; for it seemed to her often that her mind moved more quickly than theirs, and this encouraged an impatience that might easily be confounded with superiority. It may be affirmed without delay that Isabel was probably very liable to the sin of self-esteem ... Meanwhile her errors and illusions were frequently such as a biographer interested in preserving the dignity of his subject must shrink from specifying ... At moments she discovered she was grotesquely wrong, and then she treated herself to a week of passionate humility. After this she held her head higher than ever again ... The girl had a certain nobleness of imagination which rendered her a good many services and played her a great many tricks ... Sometimes she went so far as to wish that she might find herself some day in a difficult position, so that she should have the pleasure of being as heroic as the occasion demanded ...

After this our patience is invoked:

... she would be an easy victim of scientific criticism, if she were not intended to awaken on the reader's part an impulse more tender and more purely expectant. (pp. 103–5)

This passage is very often quoted, and rightly. It is full of magisterial judgement even though phrases like 'It may be affirmed ... that Isabel was probably ...' seem to distance the author from his creation and make her the free-floating figure which James so admired in Turgenev. It almost sounds like a description of one of Jane Austen's lively heroines: Marianne Dashwood in *Sense and Sensibility* or Emma in *Emma* perhaps. But an objection arises here, for, in spite of the delicate shades, qualifications and nuances of the passage it is *only* a description. Perhaps there has been no more dedicated and influential an advocate than James himself of the necessity in prose fiction to 'dramatize' the action, to show the nature of the characters through what they do and what they say as well as telling the reader, however finely, what they are like. Otherwise we would be reading a series of essays or sketches, not a novel. This familiar doctrine is expressed by Ivy Compton-Burnett, a writer said to be much influenced by James: 'I do not see why exposition and description are a necessary part of a novel. They are not of a play, and both deal with imaginary human beings and their lives' (1945). This is extreme. Yet I think it has to be admitted that although, of course, we have seen some of Isabel in the first fifty or so pages of *Portrait* we have mainly been told about her. James seems too anxious to lay his foundations, as it were, and the result is that his critique of imagination tends towards the abstract – lacks his 'blest habit of one's own imagination' in fact.

Nevertheless this point, even if the reader feels it true, may be considered as carping for two reasons. The first is that an interesting and vital similarity and contrast is being constructed in these commentaries: Ralph cannot act which is why he later makes Isabel his proxy: but he shares with her an ultimately damaging desire for freedom and for exercising his imagination:

His outward conformity to the manners that surrounded him was none the less the mask of a mind that greatly enjoyed its independence, on which nothing long imposed itself, and which, naturally inclined to adventure and irony, indulged in a boundless liberty of appreciation. (Ch. V, p. 92)

This similarity is to be crucial. Second, and even more important, the novel requires a massive initial stress on the flaws accompanying Isabel's noble charm in order to explain why she acts as she does and why she arrives at the miserable state so powerfully rendered in Chapter XLII. And these could hardly have been dramatized in fifty pages. We have to be *told* before the complex action can properly start – which it soon does. Meanwhile another important and related aspect of Isabel emerges. In the next section I shall discuss the vexed relation in this novel between liberty and marriage, particularly before marriage.

3. Fear of Experience?

Portrait, like hordes of other novels, hinges on the subject of marriage. This is, I suppose, quite natural because the choice of whom to marry or whether to marry is commonly the most important conscious, semi-conscious, or at least momentous occasion in most people's lives, and thus one of the most revealing. A hideous generalization, but it will have to serve. However, what is not often noticed, I suppose because it is so crashingly obvious, is that James is strikingly original in his time – or even, overall, in any time, including our own. There are exceptions, of course, but the dominant pattern in novels (and plays, etc.) is of a girl awaiting, in a more or less active way, an offer or offers of marriage. And Isabel explicitly is not doing so; much more explicitly not than Jane Austen's Emma (whom she resembles in more than one way) who plays with amiable complacency on the idea of celibacy but with no theoretical rigour at all. Isabel consciously rejects marriage in favour of her ideas of independence and freedom. In Chapter XV Ralph teasingly says 'Of course, if you were to marry our friend [Lord Warburton] you'd still have a career – a very decent, in fact a very brilliant one. But relatively speaking it would be a little prosaic.' To which Isabel 'abruptly' replies:

'I don't see what harm there is in my wishing not to tie myself. I don't want to begin life by marrying. There are other things a woman can do' (p. 203).This may sound like an expression of feminism, but I think it is far more a function of Isabel's complicated make-up. We can leave the feminism to Henrietta Stackpole, for Isabel is in this respect conventional and very soon adds '... I'm not an adventurous spirit. Women are not like men'. And if we look for the New Woman (a term very much in the air in those days) we shall be disappointed and find rather her idea to be in the old and honourable tradition of the active spinster – a type prominent both in life and in literature (compare the dominant Miss Carlyle in Mrs Henry Wood's *East Lynne*) and not confined to the unmarriageable. A few pages later when Caspar Goodwood surprises her by his visit to Pratt's Hotel, Isabel states her intention even more definitely (she needs to with Caspar): 'I told you just now that I don't wish to marry and that I almost certainly never shall.' She goes on to expand, in a vein now familiar, on the importance of judging for herself and wishing 'to choose my fate and know something of human affairs beyond what other people think it compatible with propriety to tell me' (Ch. XVI). This sounds much more 'adventurous' a programme than she has admitted to Ralph, but part of the point is that she is genuinely and naturally flurried and confused at this stage of the book, and, more important, does not yet know what knowledge of 'human affairs' might involve if one is not involved in them. In the previous conversation with Ralph, she has shown herself unable to take this point at all even under his definite if gentle prompting:

'... I do want to look about me.'

'You want to drain the cup of experience.'

'No, I don't wish to touch the cup of experience. It's a poisoned drink! I only want to see for myself.'

'You want to see, but not to feel.' Ralph remarked.

'I don't think that if one's a sentient being one can make the distinction.'

The question thus arises as to what it is in Isabel, apart from her youth and inexperience, that accounts for these contradictory and at first sight negative attitudes. I think it fanciful to attribute (as some critics do) very much importance to her memories of her erratic upbringing by her father: even the incident of being abandoned at Neufchâtel for three months at the age of eleven because of her *bonne's* elopement with a Russian nobleman (Ch. IV) is and was, typically, seen by her as a 'romantic episode in a liberal education'. Nevertheless the romantic or vaguely idealistic is very definitely part of her adult response to marriage and sexuality, and a part which works against acceptance. In Chapter VI (again) we are told that:

... something pure and proud that there was in her – something cold and dry an unappreciated suitor with a taste for analysis might have called it – had hitherto kept her from any great vanity of conjecture on the article of possible husbands ... Deep in her soul – it was the deepest thing there – lay a belief that if a certain light should dawn she could give herself completely: but this image, on the whole was too formidable to be attractive. Isabel's thoughts hovered about it, but they seldom rested on it long; after a little it ended in alarms.

And we return quickly to idealism of a sort: 'She often checked herself with the thought of the thousands of people who were less happy than herself' and concludes that: 'a general impression of life . . . was necessary to prevent mistakes, and after it should be secured she might make the unfortunate condition of others a subject of special attention'. (pp. 106–7)

This is admirable no doubt, and the aspiration is shared by a lot of young people often with real effect. What is peculiar to Isabel is that her vision of marriage is *opposed* in quite a rigid manner to any other worthwhile activity. At the end of her comic visit to his grand house at Lockleigh and his timid and extremely English sisters, Lord Warburton is quite obviously courting her – '. . . you've charmed me, Miss Archer'. And in modifying his sharp judgement provoked by her evasive manner and uneasy banter that 'you care only to amuse yourself', he concedes with an air of temporary humorous withdrawal that 'You select great materials; the foibles, the afflictions of human nature, the peculiarities of nations!' But she is not really appeased and this time James tells us directly why:

... her coldness was not the calculation of her effect – a game she played in a much smaller degree than would have seemed probable to many critics. It came from a certain fear. (Ch. IX, pp. 134–5)

This is the end of the chapter and so gains emphasis. And readers of James will be familiar with his manner of interjecting among his long many-claused sentences a short sharp one to startle, pull one up, and signal an especially important point. Here 'fear' has been added to 'formidable' and 'alarms'. It is a strong word, especially in the context of Warburton's gentle advances. And it colours the whole of Isabel's sexual history, if one can call it that.

A little later, when reflecting on her suitors, Warburton and Goodwood, Isabel again expresses her thoughts to herself, when weighing the former's great charms and advantages in the terminology of an admittedly half-pleasant fear – 'a certain alarm ... composed of several elements, not all of which were disagreeable' – and limitation of her freedom: in his grand 'system and orbit ... there was something stiff and stupid which would make it a burden'. As to Goodwood, she is uneasy about the force of his character (Ch. XII, p. 156). When Warburton actually proposes the language becomes quite violently metaphorical:

> But though she was lost in admiration of her opportunity she managed to move back into the deepest shade of it, even as some wild, caught creature in a vast cage. The 'splendid security' so offered was *not* the greatest she could conceive. (p. 162)

And, almost immediately, she reverts to her ideas of experience and knowledge in relation to marriage, by now a familiar dichotomy:

> She couldn't marry Lord Warburton; the idea failed to support any enlightened prejudice in favour of the free exploration of life that she had hitherto entertained or was now capable of entertaining ... But what disturbed her, in the sense that it struck her with wonderment, was this very fact that it cost her so little to refuse a magnificent 'chance'. (p. 164)

The tone is slightly ironic here ('enlightened prejudice') but what is really striking about it and the whole sequence I have been tracing – I assume the reader will have noticed it – is that while fear, freedom and idealism are constantly stressed in Isabel's reactions, there is no mention at all of a common ingredient in marriage, namely love. Isabel is certainly not mercenary; nor are the motives of those as yet around her. James was not a prude. So why this egregious absence not only of love but even of sexual attraction?

We already have fear and its cognates; already hints and demonstrations also that Isabel is not only extremely attractive to nearly all the men she meets, but, while naturally enjoying admiration, has in reserve a kind of instinctive coldness if pressed too closely. But here the commentator must fly to her rescue for such an account suggests a frigid stereotype – for describing which there is much cruder language. And the whole point is that she is manifestly not a stereotype at all, but intensely and freshly individual. A portrait is of a person, and if it is as good as this one it will suggest all the nuances that go to make up a unique creature. Art which offers an account of lives near to our day-to-day experience ('realism' as opposed to allegory, etc.) depends absolutely for its generalizable or universal quality on the individuality of its characters – which is not a paradox because any intelligent reader will soon get bored with mere types and on an off day will do well to settle firmly in front of *Dallas*, or something of tne sort, which is certainly more stereotypically colourful and entertaining and less trouble than a wooden book. (This is not a recommendation of off days, by the way.) Good novelists make us believe in their creations, make us probe their depths and care about what happens to them: which is probably why the novel is generally the most popular form of high art. Even in less realistic art, verse drama for example, this applies with force. Hamlet is individual or he is nothing.

But back to Isabel. Her charm and wit and freshness are, I find, evident to nearly every reader: they go along with the critique I have discussed, are intimately involved with it even when she is at her worst and the author at his most severe. These characteristics and others which appear later in her development should come out in subsequent discussion of specific episodes. Meanwhile, we should note that her physical attractiveness is marvellously rendered and linked with vulnerability as well as with fear, and related feelings. Consider, for example, the painful scene, painful for the reader as well as for them, with Warburton in the picture gallery at Gardencourt in Chapter XIV. This follows a delightfully comic luncheon with Henrietta Stackpole. But in the gallery he renews his wooing and dismays her:

Isabel walked to the other side of the gallery and stood there showing him her charming back, her light slim figure, the length of her white neck as she bent her head, and the density of her dark braids. She stopped in front of a small picture as if for the purpose of examining it; and there was something so young and free in her movement that her very pliancy seemed to mock at him. Her eyes, however, saw nothing; they had suddenly been suffused with tears. (p. 185)

But the real cruxes concerning Isabel's attitude to marriage are, of course, in her responses to her three suitors before her marriage, that event being the turning-point in the book. It is unnecessary to comment much further on Warburton's offer. As we have seen it *is* a magnificent 'chance' for an obscure American girl and it takes a rare person to refuse such grandeur especially when offered by so sympathetic a nobleman. In her position I would accept like a shot because I find Warburton the most admirable man in the book and am probably a snob, like Osmond. (Incidentally, although I have never seen this conjectured, I think it likely from James's letters that Warburton is partly modelled on Lord Roseberry, the future Prime Minister, with whom James was on very friendly terms at that time, and whom he admired.) But Isabel is really in love with her freedom, not him – this episode itself demonstrates with force that her talk of it is after all not mere talk – and we can believe that her acceptance would involve for her a 'cage' however vast – especially since Ralph, to a large extent a source of wisdom, agrees that 'relatively speaking it would be a little prosaic'. In George Eliot's *Daniel Deronda* (1876) the wild and sparkling Gwendoline Harleth marries the rich and aristocratic Grandcourt: but he is a sadistic egoist, at least in part a model for Osmond. And this is the classic situation. However, there is a rival tradition in literature and no doubt in life in which lively and beautiful women find themselves cramped and uneasy in unions with grandees who are not finally unsympathetic to them or to the reader: the Duchess Sanseverina in Stendhal's *La Chartreuse du Parme* and Lady Dedlock in *Bleak House*, although very different from each other, are cases in point. Here Isabel is original in that wealth and status are positive discouragements for her. She *is* an 'American girl', after all. Finally on this point it is well to notice that, as befits so important an episode, Isabel receives her first significant lesson in self-knowledge in the novel. At the end of Chapter XII after the rebuffed Warburton hurries chagrined away she reflects:

She liked him too much to marry him, that was the truth; something assured her there was a fallacy somewhere in the glowing logic of the proposition – as *he* saw it – even though she mightn't put her very finest finger-point on it; and to inflict upon a man who offered so much a wife with a tendency to criticize would be a peculiarly discreditable act. She had promised him she would consider his question . . . But this was not the case; she was wondering if she were not a cold, hard, priggish person, and, on her at last getting up and going rather quickly back to the house, felt, as she had said to her friend, really frightened at herself. (pp. 164–5)

We have been told in Chapter VI that she can be humble: now we see it. And the fear here is, importantly, not of other people.

Hard on the heels of Warburton follows his parallel and opposite, Caspar Goodwood. He, it is obvious, is the major direct sexual threat in *Portrait*. He scarcely exists as anything other than the dominant male incarnate. On hearing from him, Isabel immediately makes the relevant comparison: '. . . however she might have resisted conquest at her English suitors' large quiet hands she was at least as far removed from a disposition to let the young man from Boston take positive possession of her.' (Ch. XIII, p. 168) The juxtaposition of 'large quiet hands' and 'positive possession' tells its own story. Indeed, the imagery constantly associated with Caspar (harsh name) is sometimes so explicit that it might make our notion of the Victorian 'young person' blush – although there is no evidence that it did. Isabel does, it is true, see him as well as a kind of moral force but always in terms of aggression and rule. Thrilling perhaps, but mainly frightening. Consider some of the first metaphorical characterizations of him (these look forward to the close of the novel):

There was a disagreeably strong push, a kind of hardness of presence, in his way of rising before her. (p. 168)

[He] expressed for her an energy – and she had already felt it as a power – that was of his very nature. It was in no degree a matter of his 'advantages' – it was a matter of the spirit that sat in his clear-burning eyes like some tireless watcher at a window. She might like it or not, but he insisted, ever, with his whole weight and force . . . (p. 169)

His jaw was too square and set and his figure too straight and stiff: these things suggested a want of easy consonance with the deeper rhythms of life. (p. 170)

He showed his appetites and designs too simply and too artlessly . . . And yet he was of supremely strong, clean make – which was so much: she saw the different fitted parts of him as she had seen, in museums and portraits, the different fitted parts of armoured warriors – in plates of steel handsomely inlaid with gold. (p. 171)

I find Goodwood rather a bore, precisely because of his single-minded forcefulness. But he certainly has his rôle as an extreme in Isabel's marriage drama. We are clearly meant to register the difference in tone between her courteous interviews with Warburton and the acerbity of the conversation during Caspar's raid on Pratt's hotel. To his declaration that he is 'infernally in love' with her, Isabel replies:

'Think of me or not, as you find most possible; only leave me alone.'
'Until when?'
'Well, for a year or two.'
'Which do you mean? Between one year and two there is all the difference in the world.'
'Call it two then,' said Isabel with a studied effect of eagerness.
'And what shall I gain by that?' her friend asked with no sign of wincing.
'You'll have obliged me greatly.'
'And what will be my reward?'
'Do you need a reward for an act of generosity?'
'Yes, when it involves a great sacrifice.'
'There's no generosity without some sacrifice. Men don't understand such things. If you make the sacrifice you'll have all my admiration.'
'I don't care a cent for your admiration – not one straw, with nothing to show for it. When will you marry me? That's the only question.'

'Never – if you go on making me feel only as I feel at present.' (Ch. XVI, p. 209)

The scene does not consist solely of such grim fencing. Isabel feels, characteristically, a romanticized 'literary' sympathy for the 'strong man in pain' and tries to be gentle, as does he. But it is a hard kind of courting; a clash of wills rather than a meeting of affections. She wins in the face of this blunt attack – 'I like my liberty too much' – and the lesson she learns from it is both natural and odd. Natural in that in the midst of her subsequent exhaustion and 'tremor' she discovers the 'enjoyment she found in the exercise of her power . . . she had done something; she had tasted the delight, if not of battle, at least of victory; she had done what was truest to her plan' (Ch. XVII, p. 217). This lends further substance to the ferocity of her desire for a still as yet undefined 'theoretic' liberty. Odd in that the formidable Goodwood has proved less of a challenge than the gentle Warburton. It was the latter who, even before directly courting her, had caused 'a certain fear'. Goodwood produces triumph, tempered with pity.

So by this stage, Isabel has managed to repel boarders, and learnt a good deal. Not nearly enough however to deal with the far subtler threat which she soon faces. I shall be discussing Mme Merle and Osmond later on (see sections 5 and 6), so shall here deal only with what we might well call the latter's marriage strategy. It consists quite simply in what Isabel thinks of as 'her lover's admirable good conduct' (Ch. XXXV). By the time of his avowal of love for her the reader has been shown the ruthless duplicity which attends this (Ch. XXVI) and his egotistic conceit and coldness have been confirmed authorially (for example at the end of Ch. XXVIII). But she has experienced only his undoubted charm, his apparent distinction as a connoisseur and the modesty and dignity with which he takes the world's rejection of his fine mind and great knowledge. He seems disinterested and rare: a complex, intriguing and scrupulously kind man. All this is obvious enough; but above all for Isabel he is not in the least demanding, he does not impinge on her. Even the extremely sceptical Ralph has to concede him as seeming 'the easiest of men to live with' having 'both tact and gaiety', a 'delightful associate. His good-humour was imperturbable, his knowledge of the right fact, his production of the right word, as convenient as the friendly flicker of a match for your cigarette' (Ch. XXIX, p. 355. In his crucial late evening interview at the garish hotel in Rome in Chapter XXIX he shows all this and more: his manner is the secret of his success. An apparently desultory conversation leads to Isabel being deeply saddened that they shall part:

The sensation kept her silent, and Gilbert Osmond was silent too: he was looking at her. 'Go everywhere,' he said at last, in a low, kind voice; 'do everything; get everything out of life. Be happy – be triumphant.'
'What do you mean by being triumphant?'
'Well, doing what you like.' (p. 359)

This, of course, is marvellous for her but has a curious double-edged effect. Far from being demanding, he encourages her to be free: and this very encouragement prompts her to question the substance and point of her freedom. He then, with perfect timing, quietly declares his love. She is characteristically alarmed and stands up, but is compelled to face him:

The two remained a while in this situation, exchanging a long look – the large, conscious look of the critical hours of life. Then he got up and came near her, deeply respectful, as if he were afraid he had been too familiar. 'I'm absolutely in love with you.'
He had repeated the announcement in a tone of almost impersonal discretion, like a man who expected very little from it but who spoke for his own needed relief. (p. 360)

She cries at 'the sharpness of the pang that suggested to her somehow the slipping of a fine bolt – backward, forward, she couldn't have said which'. A beautiful sentence in itself, and of course, horribly premonitory for the reader. But she still retreats. She (of all people) feels 'the dread of having . . . to choose and decide.' But he rounds off his effect with a consummate speech:

'I haven't the idea that it will matter much to you,' said Osmond. 'I've too little to offer you. What I have – it's enough for me; but it's not enough for you. I've neither fortune, nor fame, nor extrinsic virtues of any kind. So I offer nothing. I only tell you because I think it can't offend you, and some day or other it may give you pleasure. It gives me pleasure, I assure you . . . It gives me no pain, because it's perfectly simple. For me you'll always be the most important woman in the world.' (pp. 360–1)

This is perfect: notice especially the reference to 'extrinsic virtues' which so gently advertises the intrinsic ones which he knows she thinks he has (and, for that matter, he thinks he has). The appeal is so strong that it enables Isabel to centre all her idealism on him and to ride over or survive all the subsequent hostility of her friends, even the explicit downright force of Ralph's disgust. Osmond has managed to enlist all her fine free motivations, and her fears, on his side. It is his unde-mandingness which counts. Goodwood has relied upon blunt and force-ful masculinity. Warburton, as gentle and modest as Osmond seems, is nevertheless demanding by virtue of the (for him unfortunate here) very grandeur and greatness of the position that he can offer coupled with his robust honesty and ardour. But Isabel mistakes the small for the beautiful, and accepts 'nothing', not believing that nothing *will* come of nothing in this case. Given her character and the sheer virtuosity of Osmond's campaign the result is not just plausible, but brilliantly convincing. 'Inevitable', as the critics tend to say.

4. Wind in her Sails

I now turn to one (not the sole) motive for Osmond's interest in Isabel. Her money. This entails a look at Ralph who is one of Isabel's four male admirers, though he is debarred from being a suitor. Why is he thus debarred? Looked at closely, this turns out to be a complicated question. If James wanted a sane, loving and acute observer of Isabel's career he could have used another woman (Henrietta only partly fills the rôle because of her own idiosyncrasy) or a brother, for example. Is it fair, is it profitable to the fiction, to employ instead a dying man who loves her and whom we are pretty sure she would love? Of course, there would be no story, or a very banal and short one, if Ralph were healthy. But perhaps the real answer is that he, with his combination of all that is best in Warburton, Goodwood and Osmond – wealth and gentleness, constancy and independence, taste and wit – is so *nearly* right as to add a repeated undertone of greater poignancy to the tale. We are constantly made to feel 'If only . . .' – and indeed this feeling surfaces among other things (of which more shortly) in his last interview with his father. But much earlier on, in our first full introduction to him in Chapter V just after he has met Isabel, we are told that in the face of his illness he has already come to find a kind of consolation for his disappointment of life:

With the prospect of losing them, the simple use of his faculties became an exquisite pleasure; it seemed to him the joys of contemplation had never been sounded. (p. 94)

Nevertheless his 'serenity was but the array of wild flowers niched in his ruin' and:

It was very probably this sweet-tasting property of the observed thing in itself that was mainly concerned in Ralph's quickly-stirred interest in the advent of a young lady who was evidently not insipid . . . It may be added . . . that the imagination of loving – as distinguished from that of being loved – had still a place in his reduced sketch. He had only forbidden himself the riot of expression. However, he shouldn't inspire his cousin with a passion, nor would she be able, even should she try, to help him to one. (p. 95)

So we see that Ralph's determination to renounce Isabel for himself, although James gives him impeccable medical evidence, is also an act of will. He is, though not the first, one of the most prominent of a long line of disinterested or seemingly disinterested spectators in James's *oeuvre* – persons who are frequently linked by critics to the author himself: a vulgar practice although not always implausible.

At any rate, Ralph is not at all passive in his 'joys of contemplation'. Beneath his nonchalant and bantering manner, his 'band of music', evidently lies a power of feeling, of frustration, which erupts, for example, in his discussion with her of Isabel's rejection of Warburton:

'. . . why shouldn't I speak to you of this matter without annoying you or embarrassing myself? What's the use of being your cousin if I can't have a few privileges? What's the use of adoring you without hoping for a reward if I can't have a few compensations? What's the use of being ill and disabled and restricted to mere spectatorship at the game of life if I really can't see the show when I've paid so much for my ticket?' (Ch. XV, p. 201)

What he wants, he explains when the bitterness fades, is 'the thrill of seeing what a young lady does who won't marry Lord Warburton'. Now comes the crux. Every reader will have noticed that Ralph has an imagination as avid though not so naive as Isabel's. And this results in the ultimately disastrous act – the only act he is able to perform – of giving her full licence to indulge her vaunted freedom and independence. A very large licence of £60,000. This is generous, but also complicated. Its lack of wisdom is finally revealed and acknowledged. But even at the outset a certain dubiousness attends it. On the surface Isabel gains; but is not Ralph equally or even more the benefactor of his own benefaction? Is not his judgement of her judgement (reading James tends to make one write like this, I am afraid) at fault? He has evidence that she does not mind about money in her refusal of Warburton. But he, on whom we rely for much of the intelligence and penetration in the book, cannot or will not see that her inexperienced idealism might lead to disaster. Near the end of the scene in which he persuades his dying father to leave the money to Isabel, the acute old banker, though somewhat at the mercy of his son's love, objects that 'a young lady with sixty thousand pounds may fall a victim to the fortune hunters' and receives the, when we look at it more closely, rather strange reply: 'That's a risk, and it has entered into my calculation. I think it's appreciable, but I think it's small and I'm prepared to take it' (Ch. XVIII, p. 238). Perhaps it is natural that he should not foresee Osmond. But the '*I'm* prepared to take it' forces the reader to ask, who is being put at risk? Isabel surely? – and all to satisfy Ralph's curiosity, or, as I said earlier, to allow him to live by proxy. In fact, the whole of the preceding dialogue has led up to this. Mr Touchett, who cannot be dismissed as a judge, has objected to Ralph's whole attitude to his illness and his cousin:

'You're a great deal better than you used to be. All you want is to lead a natural life. It is a great deal more natural to marry a pretty young lady that you're in love with than it is to remain single on false principles.' (pp. 234–5)

Ralph evades this by saying, surely falsely, that he is not in love. And when he proposes to 'put a little wind in her sails', his expansion 'I should like to put money in her purse' produces bafflement. James is not given much to literary allusions. But he can hardly have reminded us of Iago by accident. Ralph is no villain, yet a semi-sinister note keeps intruding. On his father's further probing he produces a famous definition: 'I call people rich when they're able to meet the requirements of their imagination. Isabel has a great deal of imagination.' (How superb to have a cousin who felt like that.) But this is followed by further discussion of the possibility of marriage for Isabel which leads Ralph into:

'It's just to do away with anything of that sort that I make my suggestion. If she has an easy income she'll never have to marry for a support. That's what I want cannily to prevent. She wishes to be free, and your bequest will make her free.' (p. 236)

Very canny indeed. Can it be that Ralph is using his generosity for a secret, only semi-conscious jealous purpose, and in affirming Isabel's freedom trying to ensure that she will not use it? In the film *The Seventh Veil*, James Mason icily spits at Anne Todd 'If you will not play [the piano] for me, you will never play for anyone else' (or words to that effect), and smashes her fingers with his cane – a great moment. Ralph is no such melodramatic figure but his father voices an unease that the alert reader should have come to feel when he says:

'You speak as if it were for your mere amusement.'
'So it is, a good deal.'
'Well, I don't think I understand,' said Mr Touchett with a sigh. 'Young men are very different from what I was. When I cared for a girl – when I was young – I wanted to do more than look at her.' (p. 237)

Finally, Ralph closes the issue with a statement so bland as to seem obtuse:

'I shall get just the good I said a few moments ago I wished to put into Isabel's reach – that of having met the requirements of my imagination. But it's scandalous, the way I've taken advantage of you!' (p. 238)

The last two words – 'of you' – have a kind of forceful bathos: we perhaps are meant to think of someone else he might be taking advantage of.

Now all this is quintessentially 'Jamesian' with its multiple suggestions and nuances. That Ralph is a good man we cannot doubt. That he makes a mistake here is equally clear. And that he is acting selfishly in a paradoxical kind of way is more than hinted at. Perhaps in his superior wisdom he is just as vulnerable to the delusions of imagination and freedom as the young Isabel. It is a complex art and very realistic, I think. Subtle, non-emphasized, *qualification* of thought and feeling (often exaggerated by critics – and sometimes actually present as in, for example, the much later *The Turn of the Screw*, *The Sacred Fount* and *The Golden Bowl* – into a celebrated or denigrated 'ambiguity') is James's characteristic stance. It is what has influenced so many subsequent writers. To pick at random among contemporary novelists here is a typical sentence from Anita Brookner's *A Start in Life* (1981):

She was in no hurry to enter the adult world, knowing in advance, and she was not wrong, that she was badly equipped for being there.

Here 'and she was not wrong' does not, I think, mean that she was *right*: and the reader is perhaps able to feel this in a way, or with an ease, the majority of James's own readers were apparently not, they being used to more certainty. Possibly this is one of the reasons why he is hailed as one of the first 'modern' writers – for better or worse.

5. Appearances

It is now time to turn from the vulnerabilities and dubieties of idealism, freedom and imagination to the more worldly world which confronts and nearly destroys them. It is clearly a very deliberate piece of timing on James's part to introduce the first important representative of this world immediately before, and in the same chapter as, the scene (just discussed) in which Ralph persuades his father to endow Isabel with the fortune which will so disastrously attract it. Mme Merle is first encountered playing the piano (Beethoven in the first publication, Schubert in the final revision – one wonders what the unmusical James had in mind here). This is the first exhibition of her very large range of gifts and accomplishments, and many others are quickly displayed. She charms Isabel even though Ralph – once allegedly in love with her – returns to his rôle as a touchstone in disliking her. Isabel is soon 'even more dazzled than attracted' and wishes to imitate her. One can easily see why: for what she has to offer is precisely what the ingenuous heroine lacks – knowledge, discernment, a cultivated tact, taste, and above all, a discreetly intimated depth of experience. All this without any show of superiority. She even, by her toleration of Henrietta's hostility, produces in Isabel a new object for idealism:

'That's the great thing,' Isabel solemnly pondered; 'that's the supreme good fortune; to be in a better position for appreciating people than they are for appreciating you.' And she added that such, when one considered it, was simply the essence of the aristocratic situation. In this light, if none other, one should aim at the aristocratic situation. (Ch. XIX, p. 242)

She is already being drawn away from her earlier ideals of the necessity for heroic suffering. Mme Merle soon becomes 'in short the most comfortable, profitable, amenable person to live with' – a phrase later ominously echoed in Ralph's concession that Osmond seemed 'the easiest of men to live with'.

However, smooth as the running continues to be, a highly significant, if slight, modification soon occurs:

If for Isabel she had a fault it was that she was not quite natural; by which the girl meant, not that she was either affected or pretentious, since from these vulgar vices no woman could have been more exempt, but that her nature had been too much overlaid by custom and her angles too much rubbed away. She had become too flexible, too useful, was too ripe and too final. She was in a word too perfectly the social animal man and woman are supposed to have been intended to be . . . (p. 244)

Too much, in short. But Isabel argues the impression away thus:

. . . her nature spoke none the less in her behaviour because it spoke a conventional tongue. 'What's language at all but a convention?' said Isabel. 'She has the good taste not to pretend, like some people I've met, to express herself by original signs.'

A glance at Henrietta or Goodwood, perhaps? But the chief and illuminating function of this apologia is that it shows us how far towards 'the world' Isabel has already come, how far she is already prepared by her new friendship to accept, unaware of its rigorous and stifling consequences and the thoroughness of its application, Osmond's later *candid* little confession that 'I'm not conventional: I'm convention itself.'

Things happen quickly to Isabel after the entry of Mme Merle. And they lead to a rightly famous discussion, often quoted because it is central to the theme of the novel. James himself calls it 'metaphysical' – about where the essential truths of life are to be found. But it occurs very naturally in the context of Mme Merle's half-teasing enquiries as to what kind of suitors Isabel has had. They are humorously chatting. But now Mme Merle launches into a general and formidable view:

'. . . every human being has his shell and . . . you must take the shell into account. By the shell I mean the whole envelope of circumstances. There's no such thing as an isolated man or woman; we're each of us made up of some cluster of appurtenances. What shall we call our "self"? Where does it begin? where does it end? It overflows into everything that belongs to us – and then it flows back again . . . I've a great respect for *things*! One's self – for other people – is one's expression of one's self; and one's house, one's furniture, one's garments, the books one reads, the company one keeps – these things are all expressive.'

This is by no means an easy argument to counter: and it is not to the present purpose to attempt a philosophical discussion. The essence of Isabel's reply is a simple unargued rebuttal:

'I don't agree with you . . . I don't know whether I succeed in expressing myself, but I know that nothing else expresses me. Nothing that belongs to me is any measure of me; everything's on the contrary a limit, a barrier, and a perfectly arbitrary one.' (Ch. XIX, p. 253)

This, the opposite extreme to Mme Merle's subtle proposition, leaves a similar sense of unease, of inconclusiveness behind the downright manner. But the whole interchange casts an ominous shadow on the future. For the external world of pure appearances is precisely that in which Isabel is to find herself when married to Osmond. The valuation of this world against that of the young Isabel is, of course, crucial to the novel.

However, we should avoid a common mistake in interpretations of *Portrait* at this point. Mme Merle is often seen simply as an agent for Osmond, charming and confusing Isabel into a state on which Osmond can work or for which he will be at least be gratified and grateful – her deeper motives appearing only later. On the contrary, a careful reading will show that there is nothing particularly scheming or underground about her presentation of herself and her 'philosophy' as yet. Her first mention of Osmond is in the context of a long and witty discourse on the fate of American expatriates in Europe in which she makes a mock denigratory comparison of him with Ralph:

'The worst case, I think, is a friend of mine . . . who is one of the most delightful men I know. Some day you must know him. I'll bring you together and then you'll see what I mean. He's Gilbert Osmond . . . He's exceedingly clever, a man made to be distinguished; but as I tell you, you exhaust the description when you say he's Mr Osmond who lives *tout bêtement* in Italy. No career, no name, no position, no past, no future, no anything.' (Ch. XIX, p. 249)

This is not quite candid, of course: but the point about it, so often overlooked, is that she is not at that moment fishing for a fortune for her ex-lover and her daughter, for the elementary reason that Isabel has no fortune and cannot seem especially likely to acquire one. It takes Ralph's fatal intervention to turn her into a real 'catch'. When she does inherit the money (now, somewhat mysteriously, £10,000 more than it was to have been) Mme Merle is so surprised as to be thrown into an uncharacteristic confusion and lets her cultivated mask slip for a moment. On Mrs Touchett's information she cries 'Ah ... the clever creature!' and has to evade Mrs Touchett's stern question 'What do you mean by that?' (Ch. XX, p. 260) with a series of skilled sophistries.

It is only then that the campaign to ensnare Isabel can be said to begin. And it does this quite explicitly for the reader, as opposed to the heroine, during our first introduction to Osmond himself in Chapter XXII. This *blasé* aesthete at first responds with what James calls 'a sort of genial crudity':

'Is she beautiful, clever, rich, splendid, universally intelligent and unprecedently virtuous? It's only on these conditions that I care to make her acquaintance ... I know plenty of dingy people; I don't want to know any more.' (p. 291)

And after some extremely inferential talk he comes 'colder and more attentive' back to Isabel's best qualification for his attention:

'Did you say she was rich?'
'She has seventy thousand pounds.'
'En écus bien comptés?'
'There's no doubt whatever about her fortune. I've seen it, as I may say.'
'Satisfactory woman – I mean, *you* ...' (p. 293)

With a final 'I want you of course to marry her', Mme Merle has done most of her work by now. Thereafter she has simply to bring the horse to water, as it were.

6. A Case for Osmond? (I)

When I asserted that Isabel's money is in Osmond's eyes her best qualification I trust that the reader bridled a bit. Money is vital all right. But it is for him only a necessary and *not* a sufficient condition. People who marry for it – or its equivalent in rank or status and so on – are perennial material for fiction, and, no doubt, common cases in life. I wonder if it sounds cynical to guess that there are, even in our enlightened and disinterested day, men who secretly – it would have to be secretly –

regret the passing of the Married Woman's Property Act in 1881 by which the husband was prevented from automatically becoming master of his wife's fortune. Be that as it may, it was just about this time that three distinguished English novels have as one of their main themes the subduing of a spirited and beautiful girl to the will of a cold, calculating and vain husband: *Portrait* itself, Meredith's *The Egoist* (1879), and as I have mentioned George Eliot's *Daniel Deronda* (1876). In the latter two, money is not the issue for the men – what they want is dominance and possession. We might compare the hints as to Osmond given by his creation of the perfect, obedient, decorative and almost robotic *jeune fille* in Pansy with the wonderful scene in Chapter XII of *Daniel Deronda* where Grandcourt before *his* marriage is seen at breakfast with his sycophant, Mr Lush:

... Fetch, the beautiful liver-coloured water-spaniel ... sat with its fore-paws firmly planted and its expressive brown face turned upward, watching Grandcourt with unshaken constancy.

He snubs her by playing with a tiny Maltese toy dog. She puts her paw on his leg:

Grandcourt looked at her with unchanged face for half a minute then took the trouble to lay down his cigar while he lifted the unimpassioned Fluff close to his chin and gave it caressing pats, all the while gravely watching Fetch, who, poor thing, whimpered interruptedly, as if trying to repress that sign of discontent and at last rested her head beside the appealing paw, looking up with piteous beseeching ... But when the amusing anguish burst forth in a howling bark, Grandcourt pushed Fetch down without speaking ...

She begins to howl:

'Turn out that brute, will you?' said Grandcourt to Lush, without raising his voice or looking at him – as if he counted on attention to the smallest sign.

There could hardly be a more potent image of sadistic coldness – Lush receives the same arrogant treatment as Fetch – and the passage is far more powerful and chilling a warning, I think, than any in *Portrait*. Nevertheless Grandcourt is a more thoroughly vicious man than Osmond and what especially enriches a reading of the novel is the recognition that its 'villain' has a certain case to be made in his favour. He too – leaving aside the money question – wants to dominate the young and beautiful but for reasons which have at least a certain respectability.

To begin with it is clear from his sardonic reply to Mme Merle's first mention of Isabel that riches are one consideration among many in a wife. A candidate for his attention would also have to be beautiful, clever, splendid, intelligent and virtuous. If we think this a bit of a flourish on his part, we should also ask whether we can imagine him courting an ugly, vulgar, loose girl. The answer is obviously 'no'. Such a person would not be the kind of ornament which his vision of himself, and his vision of the vision of other people could tolerate. He is consistently a perfectionist in his own terms. He has also a line in self-deprecation, which, while it contains implied self-advertisement and is clearly meant to charm, we have no reason to think of as insincere. For instance, his account of living in Italy is summarized thus:

Certain impressions you could get only there. Others, favourable to life, you never got, and you got some that were very bad. But from time to time you got one of a quality that made up for everything. Italy, all the same, had spoiled a great many people; he was even fatuous enough to believe at times that he himself might have been a better man if he had spent less of his life there. It made one idle and dilettantish and second-rate; it had no discipline for the character, didn't cultivate in you, otherwise expressed, the successful social and other 'cheek' that flourished in Paris and London ... (Ch. XXIV, p. 308)

Not that Osmond has the slightest intention of leaving Italy, as we learn. But James is not presenting a simple person. The point of such characters as Daniel Touchett, Lord Warburton and Henrietta Stackpole is that they are as clear and straightforward as could be. But, as I have argued in the case of Mme Merle, the fact that Isabel is being manipulated and used does not preclude the 'villains' from having their genuine side. This is sharply illustrated in a passage which is quoted with boring frequency as proof that Osmond is an egotist of quite grotesque pretensions:

'I had no prospects, I was poor, and I was not a man of genius. I had no talents even: I took my measure early in life. I was simply the most fastidious young gentleman living. There were two or three people in the world I envied – the Emperor of Russia, for instance, and the Sultan of Turkey! There were even moments when I envied the Pope of Rome – for the consideration he enjoys. I should have been delighted to be considered to that extent, but since that couldn't be, I didn't care for anything less.' (Ch. XXIV, p. 315)

Of course this is calculated to play on Isabel's sympathies, and it succeeds:

This would have been rather a dry account of Mr Osmond's career if Isabel had fully believed it; but her imagination supplied the human element which she was sure had not been wanting. (p. 316)

One can always rely on Isabel's imagination. But, although there may be an undercurrent of truth in Osmond's account of his ridiculous attitude, surely only a failure to respond at all to his tone can explain the willingness of readers to interpret it as a solemn indictment. He is ruefully parodying himself – poking fun at the absurdities of the 'fastidious young gentleman' of his past. Can we really believe Isabel would be other than repelled if she took him literally?

Osmond's fetching charm is, then, firmly established. If it were not, the novel would become ridiculous. It operates in counterpoint with his darker side, as when, shortly after the episode just discussed, he talks Isabel over with Mme Merle:

'The girl's not disagreeable,' Osmond quietly conceded.

Mme Merle dropped her eyes on him for a moment, during which her lips closed with a certain firmness. 'Is that all you can find to say about that fine creature?'

'All? Isn't it enough? Of how many people have you heard me say more?' (Ch. XXVI, p. 334)

Even in this slightly chilling interchange we note that Mme Merle insists on Isabel's being a 'fine creature'; there is no mention of money. It is followed by an exhibition on Osmond's part of a deeper ruthlessness:

'I like her very much. She's all you described her, and into the bargain capable, I feel, of great devotion. She has only one fault.'

'What's that?'

'Too many ideas.'

'I warned you she was clever.'

'Fortunately they're very bad ones,' said Osmond.

'Why is that fortunate?'

'*Dame*, if they must be sacrificed!' (p. 335)

Nasty: and soon authorially confirmed in Osmond's pleasure in the knowledge that Isabel has refused an English lord – a pleasure which reflects back more realistically on his ridicule of his Czar/Sultan/Pope fantasy:

Gilbert Osmond had a high appreciation of this particular patriciate; not so much for its distinction, as for its solid actuality. He had never forgiven his star for not appointing him to an English dukedom, and he could measure the unexpectedness of such a conduct as Isabel's. It would be proper that the woman he might marry should have done something of that sort. (Ch. XXVIII, p. 354)

It is not in itself uncommon or unpleasant to have day-dreams of wealth and inherited prestige. But to take them so seriously is altogether too much. However, two pages on from this we are given a rather less hostile account of the same theme:

The desire to have something or other to show for his 'parts' – to show somehow or other – had been the dream of his youth; but as the years went on the conditions attached to any marked proof of rarity had affected him more and more as gross and detestable; like the swallowing of mugs of beer to advertise what one could 'stand' . . . His 'style' was what the girl had discovered with a little help; and now, beside herself enjoying it, she should publish it to the world without his having any of the trouble. (Ch. XXIX, p. 356)

A sense of failure, of waste, and a consequent disdainful withdrawal into a self-imposed idle exclusiveness are not, I think, entirely unsympathetic. In a different context they might be material for a compassionate study. And it is important to note that Osmond sincerely believes that Isabel will herself enjoy the projected process. After all, at this point she shares it. It takes two to tango, as Osmond would not say.

Given these complexities – and there are many other instances – I find it difficult to label Osmond as simply the exploitative villain who might be (often is) found in lesser novels. As we shall see, these continue after the marriage. He is consistently what he is, and does not, for example, suddenly turn into a violent or faithless brute after he has by deception gained his prize. A final and authoritative confirmation of these points can be taken from Chapter XXXV which describes the state of the betrothed couple in the face of the hostility which their action has provoked:

Gilbert Osmond was in love, and he had never deserved less than during these still, bright days . . . which preceded the fulfilment of his hopes, the harsh criticism passed upon him by Ralph Touchett. (p. 400)

Again:

What could be a finer thing to live with than a high spirit attuned to softness? For would not the softness be all for one's self, and the strenuousness for society, which admired the air of superiority? (p. 401)

If he is not fully honest about the influence on his state of Isabel's fortune he does discuss it. He is also so convinced of the beauty of the situation for them both that, in thinking of the antagonism of her friends, he is able, possibly deceived by his own egoism, to console himself sincerely with the thought that 'he had always treated her so completely as an independent person' – and by this he obviously does not mean merely financial independence. We believe avowals such as the following because he obviously believes them himself:

'It has made me better, loving you . . . it has made me wiser and easier and – I won't pretend to deny – brighter and nicer and even stronger. I used to want a great many things before and to be angry I didn't have them. Theoretically I was satisfied, as I once told you. I flattered myself I had limited my wants. But I was subject to irritation; I used to have morbid, sterile, hateful fits of hunger, of desire. Now I'm really satisfied, because I can't think of anything better . . . We've got what we like – to say nothing of having each other. We've the faculty of admiration and several capital convictions. We're not stupid, we're not mean, we're not under bonds to any kind of ignorance or dreariness . . .' (pp. 402–3)

These are surely the utterances of genuine conviction and affection; and, as Isabel later remarks to herself, he is as much taken in by her eager acceptance of the rôle he proposes to her as she is by his presentation of it.

There is, I feel, a certain tension or strain in the novel here, and later. This may be because Osmond became more interesting and complex to his creator than his function in the book demanded: characters getting out of authorial control are quite a common phenomenon in art – the classic example, as I have mentioned, being Satan in *Paradise Lost*, but there are lots of others. Or it may be because James wanted wide recognition and had constantly been accused of not having a 'story' by his contemporaries, of being 'bloodless' and unexciting – and so wished to create a real villain. In any case I feel that the revelation of Osmond's murky past is something of a flaw in the book, though it is handled with great *finesse*. In spite of what can be said in his favour, he is, especially later on, so marvellously rendered as a cold and constricting presence that we do not need the Countess Gemini's account in Chapter LI of his previous adultery and a slight suspicion of murder. In short, he is bad enough as it is without being criminal or semi-criminal. James is perhaps here again being influenced by the powerful figure of Grandcourt in *Daniel Deronda*. And I would further argue that this late revealed villainy, with its whiff of slight implausibility, weakens our concentration on his present and powerful nastiness, rather than the reverse.

7. Parallels and Contrasts

The reader may object that in tracing the descriptions, thoughts, speech and actions of the main protagonists up to the marriage (Isabel, Ralph, Mme Merle and Osmond) and only mentioning in passing the other characters I have not done justice to the richness of texture which is so salient a feature of *Portrait*. Such an objection is valid since the interplay of character and opinion is indeed vital to the novel. Let us therefore look at some examples of it.

The roles of Lord Warburton and Caspar Goodwood are sufficiently clear as to need no further comment. But what about Henrietta? She appears early and has an obvious place as both comparison and contrast to Isabel. In his Preface (written, it must be remembered, twenty-seven years later) James apologizes for her 'super-abundance' as a person of 'whom we have indubitably too much'. She was, he says, meant to be only a 'light *ficelle*' but got out of hand. *Ficelle* is a useful critical term, promoted by James to mean a peripheral figure with a function but no substantial presence of its own. The note in the Penguin edition translates it as 'thread or attachment' but this is virtually meaningless and its further sense of 'stage-struck' with a connotation of puppeteering is very much nearer to what James had in mind. Nevertheless I do not see any reason except his later theories of artistic economy for the apology. Henrietta is an American girl like Isabel. Like Isabel, she has very strong feelings about independence and the threat posed to this by European customs generally and marriage customs in particular. And she too marries a European. But the piquancy of this overall similarity is that it is employed entirely to dramatize differences – perhaps to show what Isabel might have been were Isabel not uniquely Isabel. Henrietta is in a way a living embodiment of a cliché – while remaining comic and like-able. All this is made very clear early on, in Chapter VI:

Henrietta was in the van of progress and had clear-cut views on most subjects; her cherished desire had long been to come to Europe and write a series of letters to the *Interviewer* from the radical point of view – an enterprise the less difficult as she knew perfectly in advance what her opinions would be and to how many objections most European institutions lay open. (p. 106)

This prepares for the comedy of her first failure to get an invitation to Lady Pensil's in Bedfordshire and, indeed, for her whole relationship with the charmingly simple Mr Bantling. But the initial emphasis is on both the tactless candour and the degrees of percipience, or lack of it, which she brings to her critique of Isabel and of expatriates in general. James intensely disliked and despised popular journalists – many of his nastiest minor characters such as Matthias Pardon in *The Bostonians* (1886) and Mr Flack in *The Reverberator* (1888) being of this, for him distinctly American, species. (One boggles at what he would have thought of today's press, just as one boggles on reading a severe critique by John Stuart Mill on the meretriciousness of advertising written in 1835.) So it is something of a surprise that there is so little acerbity in his criticism of Henrietta. When she proposes to publicize the lives of

Mr Touchett and Ralph, Isabel says, 'My poor Henrietta . . . you've no sense of privacy':

> Henrietta coloured deeply and for a moment her brilliant eyes were suffused, while Isabel found her more than ever inconsequent. 'You do me great injustice,' said Miss Stackpole with dignity. 'I've never written a word about myself!'
> 'I'm very sure of that: but it seems to me one should be modest for others also!'
> 'Ah, that's very good!' cried Henrietta, seizing her pen again. 'Just let me make a note of it and I'll put it somewhere.' (Ch. X, pp. 140–1)

Henrietta is irrepressible, but in a way which makes her lovable rather than intolerable. Nevertheless this kind of thing – and there is a good deal of it, especially in her conversations with Ralph – should alert us to the fact that while she is a candid, she is by no means an infallible critic of her friend. It is particularly important to remember this in reading her important speech about Isabel's illusions in Chapter XX – a speech which is often quoted out of context as an authoritative description and prediction:

> 'I hope you'll never become grossly sensual; but I'm not afraid of that. The peril for you is that you live too much in the world of your own dreams. You're not enough in contact with reality – with the toiling, striving, suffering, I may even say sinning, world that surrounds you. You're too fastidious; you've too many graceful illusions . . . Whatever life you lead you must put your soul into it . . . And you can't always please yourself; you must sometimes please other people. That, I admit, you're very ready to do; but there's another thing that's still more important – you must often *dis*please others . . . You must be prepared on many occasions in life to please no one at all – not even yourself. (pp. 267–8)

The first part of this is fair enough, in spite of Isabel's former notions about doing good to the downcast. But of the second, which also smacks of autobiography, it is rarely noticed that Isabel is already prepared to put her soul into leading her life, so much so that she does indeed displease people and persists heroically in it. The only trouble is that she chooses the wrong thing (or person) to commit herself to.

Ralph too, before her engagement, is a commentator on his cousin. But his attitude as the narrator tells us 'though it was contemplative and critical, was not judicial'. He is not so provincial and positive as Henrietta; and he is in his strange way in love. He thus crucially though not crudely overestimates Isabel's power to resist the dangers attendant on the possession of £70,000 (which were what provoked Henrietta's speech)

45

and, as we have seen, has a curious mixture of motives in seeing that she gets that money – one of which being that he shares many of her ideas and ideals. But when Osmond succeeds his attitude changes. Before their showdown in Chapter XXIV Isabel takes a rather light and novelletish attitude to what he is likely to feel:

> . . . it would be indeed his natural line – to find fault with any step she might take towards marriage. One's cousin always pretended to hate one's husband; that was traditional, classical; it was part of one's cousin's always pretending to adore one . . . (p. 389)

This is rather silly in itself, the product of deluded happiness. It is also an index of her total failure to recognize Ralph's feelings towards her and of his success in masking them. That he is now forced to drop the mask becomes, therefore, all the more momentous. The conversation is long and on Ralph's part initially conducted with reluctance:

> 'You're beating about the bush, Ralph. You wish to say you don't like Mr Osmond, and yet you're afraid.'
> '"Willing to wound and yet afraid to strike"? I'm willing to wound *him*, yes – but not to wound you. I'm afraid of you, not of him. If you marry him it won't be a fortunate way for me to have spoken.' (Ch. XXIV, p. 393)

Ralph's reference to Pope is apt, if too severe on himself:

> Damn with faint praise, assent with civil leer,
> And, without sneering, teach the rest to sneer,
> Willing to wound, and yet afraid to strike,
> Just hint of fault and hesitate dislike.
> (*Epistle to Dr Arbuthnot*)

He is indeed hesitant to condemn outright, although not for the reasons Pope attributes to Addison. 'I know him very little, and I confess I haven't facts and items to prove him a villain,' he equivocates, and then more forthrightly, 'I believed you'd marry a man of more importance.' The reader will no doubt remember his position of self-appointed observer of what Isabel will 'do', his half-expressed desire that she shall not marry, and the sense in which he sees her as living her life as a kind of proxy for his. If not, James takes care to remind us (he is always a solicitous guide through his own labyrinths):

> 'You were not to come down so easily or so soon.'
> 'Come down, you say?'

'Well, that renders my sense of what has happened to you. You seemed to me to be soaring far up in the blue – to be sailing in the bright light, over the heads of men. Suddenly someone tosses up a faded rosebud – a missile that should never have reached you – and straight you drop to the ground. It hurts me,' said Ralph audaciously, 'hurts me as if I'd fallen myself!' (p. 395)

His 'audacious' conclusion is perhaps a piece of regretful self-knowledge. Certainly it provokes an acute rebuke from Isabel – 'You say you amused yourself with a project for my career – I don't understand that. Don't amuse yourself too much, or I shall think you're doing it at my expense.' This must hit a very painful nerve in Ralph – more painful than she can be aware of. Certainly it leads to the abandonment, possibly to the reader's relief, of the delicate metaphorical language with which he has been softening his criticism. Proceeding to the question of Osmond's taste he asks, 'But have you ever seen such a taste – a really exquisite one – ruffled?' Her reply that she hopes always to gratify Osmond's leads him into an entirely uncharacteristic and drastic directness with her:

... a sudden passion leaped to Ralph's lips. 'Ah, that's wilful, that's unworthy of you! You were not meant to be measured in that way – you were meant for something better than to keep guard over the sensibilities of a sterile dilet-tante!'
Isabel rose quickly and he did the same, so that they stood for a moment looking at each other as if he had flung down a defiance or an insult. (p. 396)

Well, he *has* thrown down an insult. The faded rosebud turns out to be a sterile dilettante. It is often the case, as I said earlier, that gentle metaphor in James is succeeded with great effect by blunt or even brutal language. And Ralph has to justify himself with equal directness, '"I love you"' – quickly amended so as not to provoke her further with '"but I love you without hope" . . . forcing a smile . . .'

A lot of the drama in this scene is produced by an irony which is central to the book: that Isabel cannot know the reasons for Ralph's special bitterness, and that he cannot tell her. If he did, which is hardly conceivable, the situation would be even more shameful and distressing than it is. So she continues to rub salt into the wound without meaning to:

'I've fortunately money enough; I've never felt so thankful for it as today. There have been moments when I should like to go and kneel down by your father's grave: he did perhaps a better thing than he knew when he put it into my power to marry a poor man – a man who has borne his poverty with such dignity, with such indifference.' (p. 397)

Ouch: he remembers, as do we, 'what he had said to his father about wishing to put it into her power to meet the requirements of her imagination. He had done so, and the girl had taken full advantage of the luxury. Poor Ralph felt sick; he felt ashamed' (pp. 398–9). The vaunted imagination on which both of them placed so much value has proved a very fallible instrument indeed: and its results will soon prove to be a mutual torment.

At this point too we may remember that there is in Isabel's eyes only a fine (though in fact crucial) distinction between the 'dilettante' natures of Osmond and Ralph. Earlier she has compared them in these terms:

> Ralph had something of this same quality, this appearance of thinking that life is a matter of connoisseurship; but in Ralph it was an anomaly, a kind of humorous excrescence, whereas in Mr Osmond it was the keynote, and everything was in harmony with it. (Ch. XXIV, p. 312)

No wonder that under Osmond's carefully wrought spell she has forgotten this distinction, together with many of her earlier ideals, and thus finds Ralph's reaction the more offensive. It is a part of the elaborate series of misunderstandings from which the action derives its power. Misunderstandings are at the centre of many novels, as they are of many situations in life.

There are many other such contrasts and parallels in the novel, enhancing the texture with a series of 'might have beens' and making the reader reflect back on the interplay of characters. I have already mentioned Mr Touchett's dry reflection that Isabel reminds him of his wife as a young woman: and this, seemingly far-fetched at the time, turns out by the end to be nearer to the truth than could have been imagined, though by no means identical with it. We are left with another estranged pair coupled only by convention. Again, while Henrietta's case is obvious, Pansy's is not and repays close attention. When she is first introduced Pansy is in absolute contrast with everyone surrounding her. James endows her with pathetic charm right from the start. Her formal ignorance about the world goes with a real innocence which is not to be confused with stupidity:

> 'Oh yes, I obey very well,' cried Pansy with soft eagerness, almost boastfulness, as if she had been speaking of her piano-playing. And then she gave a faint, just audible sigh. (Ch. XXII, p. 286)

She could not be less like her ultra-sophisticated father or Mme Merle. They, and he especially, have created her as 'a blank page, a pure white surface' – a Continental type that fascinated James and which he usually treats with compassion and a great sense of their vulnerability, their having been reared almost like fine pedigree animals for the highest bidder in the marriage market. This is made explicit in a splendid passage in *The Awkward Age* (1899) where the benign Mr Longdon reflects upon a similar case to Pansy's, in relation to that of the heroine, Nanda, who has not been so mercilessly protected and knows something of the world:

Little Aggie differed from any young person he had ever met in that she had been deliberately prepared for consumption and in that, furthermore, the gentleness of her spirit had immensely helped the preparation. Nanda, beside her, was a northern savage . . . Both the girls struck him as lambs with the great shambles of life in their future; but while one, with its neck in a pink ribbon, had no consciousness but that of being fed from the hand with the small sweet biscuit of unobjectionable knowledge, the other struggled with instincts and forebodings, with the suspicion of its doom and the far-borne scent, in the flowery fields, of blood. (Ch. 18)

When Little Aggie marries, or, rather is married, she quickly becomes silly, fast, and odiously 'knowing'. No such devastating language is applied to Pansy and she is unlikely to suffer so politely inhuman a fate, thanks to the matured Isabel. But at the same time as casting further light on the application of Osmond's cherished conventions she offers, like Henrietta, only the other way round, a finely calculated comparison and contrast with Isabel. Both are innocent: but in Isabel this is the result of freedom to range around and to experience; in Pansy the result of exclusion and confinement. Both are devoid of cunning, artless – and both eventually the victims of calculating egotism. But this is the result of choice for Isabel, the result of birth and upbringing in Pansy. Perhaps what saves Pansy is her charming, modest intelligence, a quality which Isabel underestimates at first because of her own swiftly gathering admiration for Osmond. Pansy:

. . . had neither art, nor guile, nor temper, nor talent – only two or three small exquisite instincts: for knowing a friend, for avoiding a mistake, for taking care of an old toy or a new frock . . . She would have no will, no power to resist, no sense of her own importance . . . (Ch. XXX, p. 366)

This is partly accurate but a rather special quality – precocity in an *attractive* form – immediately reveals itself in Pansy's speech, and interests the reader more than Isabel's summary would suggest:

. . . 'I'm really as yet only a child. Oh, yes, I've only the occupations of a child. When did *you* give them up, the occupations of a child? I should like to know how old you are, but I don't know whether it's right to ask. At the convent they told us that we must never ask the age. (p. 367)

This deprecating self-consciousness actually constitutes a kind of strength, as we later see. Pansy resembles Maisie in *What Maisie Knew* (1897) more than she does Little Aggie. But for the present purpose we see her mainly as a brilliantly created foil for Isabel.

Discussion of Pansy of course provokes thoughts of Mr Rosier. He too is a fine minor creation who provides the reader with comparisons and side-views on the central figures. He is seen initially in relation to both Isabel and Ralph and, more remotely because the difference is so clear, Henrietta and Caspar Goodwood. He, and the whole of the Parisian American set to which he belongs, are the objects initially of a tolerant satire (no doubt based on James's observations when he lived in Paris) on the mildly purposeless life of expatriates. Thus he reminds us emphatically of what Ralph has *not* become (in spite of Henrietta's drastic opinions). Like Pansy he has learnt 'that one must always obey' as a child. And though his father is dead and his *bonne* dismissed:

> ... the young man still conformed to the spirit of their teaching – he never went to the edge of the lake. There was still something agreeable to the nostrils about him and something not offensive to nobler organs. He was a very gentle and gracious youth, with what are called cultivated tastes – an acquaintance with old china, with good wine ... (Ch. XX, p. 265)

Thus Rosier is perfectly in equilibrium with Pansy and, like her, with more fibre and strength than is at first suggested (as we shall see). By contrast Isabel *is* prepared to plunge into the metaphorical lake of experience. But an even more subtle dramatic relation is that with Osmond himself. Both are collectors and dilettante expatriates, both poor in comparison with the Touchetts. But Rosier is humble (see the charming declaration of his own inadequacy to Isabel in Chapter XX, pp. 266–7) whereas Osmond is dominated by pride. Rosier is capable of sacrificing connoisseurship to feeling, whereas Osmond, however genuinely he feels, succeeds in collecting more and more possessions both artistic and human.

These things are obvious even to the casual reader, and therefore require little more commentary. The important point about them is that they emphasize how very closely the novel is organized, how it achieves a density of internal reference which permits practically nothing to be irrelevant to its main themes. Even, as a final example, the Countess Gemini (in addition to her main function in the plot – the revelation of Osmond's and Mme Merle's past) has a thematic use. She opposes vulgarity to her brother's refinement; she too is the victim of a stultifying marriage; she tells the truth where Osmond and Mme Merle and even

Isabel rely on keeping up appearances – 'You say things to me that no one else does' remarks Mme Merle at the beginning of a superbly bitchy piece of feminine fencing in Chapter XXV; and it is interesting to note that the mainly hostile attitude towards her which is usually registered is largely mediated through the reflections of the still idealistic Isabel. She is often underestimated.

But now it is time to turn from what is established so elaborately yet clearly before Isabel's marriage to its results: to the climax and the still, after a hundred years, debatable conclusion: to, in fact, the point and meaning of the novel.

III After Marriage

1. Prelude

Chapter XLII is, as I have said, a watershed in *Portrait*. After it events accelerate wonderfully. 'I believe the interest goes *crescendo* to the end,' remarked James to his friend T. S. Perry in January 1881 (*Letters*, Vol. II, p. 335). Most readers would agree. But first it is worth considering the function of the chapters which immediately precede Isabel's late-night vigil. In Chapter XXXVI we soon learn that the marriage has taken place and time elapsed. Then there follows a retrospective review, as it were, of reactions to it and a dramatization of how Mr and Mrs Osmond appear now: a subtle prelude to the internal revelations which follow.

James starts in a minor and humorous mode. The 'little' Mr Rosier has fallen in love with Pansy and seeks help in his courtship. He goes at first to Mme Merle as a friend of the family, and the state of his feelings is described in a tone of benign irony. Pansy has 'struck him as exactly the household angel he had long been looking for'; his 'passion' emboldens him to brave malaria in Rome – 'there was a strain of the heroic in the enterprise' – and confirm his impressions of Pansy. He does so from a point of view which is a kind of pastiche of Osmond's attitudes, and confirms Osmond's success with his daughter's upbringing:

She was admirably finished; she had had the last touch; she was really a consummate piece. He thought of her in amorous meditation a good deal as he might have thought of her Dresden-china shepherdess. Miss Osmond, indeed, in the bloom of her juvenility, had a hint of the rococo . . . (p. 409)

This view of the ideally feminine is a highly etiolated version – Rosier's aestheticized version – of the 'angel in the house', a familiar figure in nineteenth-century fiction, even in that by distinguished woman writers such as George Eliot or Charlotte Brontë. It is nowadays usually found ludicrous or odious or both, often in a simple-minded and a-historical way. James, as we have seen, is extremely sceptical of it. And in this case the dehumanization which may seem to hover in the wings is alleviated by the wit and by a sense of the mildness of the whole procedure. Rosier does not pose a threat in the way in which a more considerable man with these attitudes might have done, and his tepidity and modest intelligence as well as his modest means and lack of a title are appropriately paralleled in the lukewarmness of Mme Merle's reception. However, the chapter serves another, more important, purpose. It gives the first, rather chilling, glimpses of the Osmond marriage. Rosier believes that Isabel 'would favour me':

> 'Very likely, if her husband doesn't.'
> He raised his eyebrows. 'Does she take the opposite line from him?'
> 'In everything. They think quite differently.' (p. 411)

Later he is warned: 'I advise you not to multiply points of difference between them.' And this leads to his reflections on the Palazzo Roccanera as a 'dungeon' in which he imagines, melodramatically but prophetically perhaps, that 'at picturesque periods young girls had been shut up . . . to keep them from their true loves, and then, under the threat of being thrown into convents, had been forced into unholy marriages.' (pp. 415–16).

This vision turns into something like possible reality when in the next chapter we see the married couple at home. Osmond is memorably pictured. He:

> . . . stood before the chimney, leaning back with his hands behind him; he had one foot up and was warming the sole. Half a dozen persons, scattered near him, were talking together; but he was not in the conversation; his eyes had an expression, frequent with them, that seemed to represent them as engaged with objects more worth their while than the appearances actually thrust upon them. (Ch. XXXVII, p. 417)

He gives an abstracted left hand (rather insulting) to Rosier and, on the latter's courageous insistence, converses. Rosier offers a pathetic opening, as between collectors:

> 'I saw a jolly good piece of Capo di Monte to-day,' he said.
> Osmond answered nothing at first; but presently, while he warmed his boot-sole, 'I don't care a fig for Capo di Monte!' he returned.
> 'I hope you're not losing your interest?'
> 'In old pots and plates? Yes, I'm losing my interest.'
> Rosier for an instant forgot the delicacy of his position. 'You're not thinking of parting with a – a piece or two?'
> 'No, I'm not thinking of parting with anything at all, Mr Rosier,' said Osmond, with his eyes still on the eyes of his visitor.
> 'Ah, you want to keep, but not to add,' Rosier remarked brightly.
> 'Exactly. I've nothing I wish to match.' (p. 418)

Poor Rosier; he is still, although in love, unable to repress the collector's impulse. But Osmond has elevated himself to the status of a human refrigerator, a kind of jumped-up Grandcourt, and equally unpleasant. Why does the warming of a boot-sole seem the indication of casually brutal indifference? Perhaps because only the master of the house, demonstrating his mastery, could do it in a large gathering. At any rate the exchange is one of the most effective snubs in literature.

The evening is not pure misery for Rosier, for his muted approach to Pansy assures him, mutedly, of her love. But the episode leads back again to the state of Isabel. Trying to console him in a calm, kindly way she provokes a natural protest which must be acutely painful to her:

> 'She doesn't care a straw for one's money.'
>
> 'No, but her father does.'
>
> 'Ah yes, he has proved that!' cried the young man.

His apology for this at last breaks her cultivated reserve:

> 'I referred to Mr Osmond as I shouldn't have done, a while ago,' he began. 'But you must remember my situation.'
>
> 'I don't remember what you said,' she answered coldly.
>
> 'Ah, you're offended and now you'll never help me.'
>
> She was silent an instant, and then with a change of tone; 'It's not that I won't; I simply can't!' Her manner was almost passionate. (p. 426)

It is thus that James uses the minor comi/tragedy of Rosier and Pansy to indicate for the first time openly the awfulness of the Osmonds' marriage and the nature of Osmond's cold dominance. After it we get, naturally and artfully, a gathering of the shades: Lord Warburton and Ralph appear. Mrs Touchett's opinions are described. She thinks the marriage a 'shabby affair' and with her own brand of high logic distances herself from it and all that is connected with it – especially from her friend Mme Merle. Warburton remains important because he, in the confusion of his feelings, acts well, and of course could still be a great 'catch' for Osmond as his daughter's suitor, a great magnate who has been most gratifyingly rejected by his wife. Warburton is in a state of pleasant uneasiness, reducing, without meaning to, any ease that Rosier may have felt. This intrigue is clear and although intricate needs little comment. Much more important is Ralph's reaction. He analyses painfully the sources of pain. At first he can only go on impressions, being cut off from intimacy with Isabel precisely because he had been so right about Osmond. Now he is naturally reluctant to claim any kind of victory. He cannot get behind the 'fixed and mechanical . . . serenity' of her mask, cannot even comfort her about the loss of her child (this child being, I think, a rather arbitrary functional addition by James – depriving Isabel of compensation and leading on, *if* we remember it, to an added sense of responsibility for Pansy). But his guesswork is devastating and a perfect preparation for Isabel's self-revelations. Its most interesting feature is that he sees that the 'studied impressions' given off by Mr and Mrs Osmond's impressively reticent and exclusive 'magnificence' are a creation by Osmond himself – not by her; he 'recognized the hand of the master'. And, correspondingly, she has declined and outwardly *coarsened*:

She struck him as having a great love of movement, of gaiety, of late hours, of long rides, of fatigue; an eagerness to be entertained, to be interested, even to be bored, to make acquaintances, to see people who were talked about ... etc. (Ch. XXXIX, p. 443)

These signs of emptiness, dissipation, or even desperation are naturally compared with the past Isabel, the girl with all the world before her whom he has endowed with the money to make her perfectly 'free':

There was a kind of violence in some of her impulses, of crudity in some of her experiments, which took him by surprise: it seemed to him that she even spoke faster, moved faster, breathed faster, than before her marriage. Certainly she had fallen into exaggerations – she who used to care so much for the pure truth; and whereas of old she had a great delight in good-humoured argument, in intellectual play ... she appeared now to think there was nothing worth people's either differing about or agreeing upon. Of old she had been curious, and now she was indifferent ... (pp. 443–4)

She even looks different: 'The free keen girl had become ... the fine lady who was supposed to represent something.' She represents, of course, Osmond. '"Good heavens, what a function!" he then woefully exclaimed. He was lost in wonder at the mystery of things.' This is a fine analysis, confirming completely what we have seen of her in her dealings with poor Rosier. In addition the dramatic balance is extremely delicate since although we believe Ralph's account we simultaneously realize that it is from his point of view only, near to the author's but not identical with it. He, for instance, still rather idealizes the younger Isabel, and it is curious that, having previously been so piercing about Osmond's nature ('sterile dilettante'), he should find the result of the marriage a part of the 'mystery of things'.

Turning to Osmond himself Ralph is even more imaginately perceptive:

... under the guise of caring only for intrinsic values Osmond lived exclusively for the world. Far from being its master as he pretended to be, he was its very humble servant, and the degree of its attention was his only measure of success. He lived with his eye on it from morning till night, and the world was so stupid it never suspected the trick. Everything he did was *pose – pose* so subtly considered that if one were not on the lookout one mistook it for impulse . . . His ambition was not to please the world, but to please himself by exciting the world's curiosity and then declining to satisfy it. (pp. 444–5)

This is splendidly sensitive and convincing, so much so that it is often treated as definitive. That it is not, the subsequent thoughts and behaviour of both Isabel and Osmond will show. Nevertheless it is very easy to miss a direct hint from James that Ralph, as I have remarked, is not the voice of the novel but a character in it:

> I give this little sketch of its [Ralph's 'creed'] articles for what they may at the time have been worth. It was certain that he was very skilful in fitting the facts to his theory . . . (p. 445)

The progression of revelations now gathers pace. On the plane of the obvious Osmond grows even more odious. He has a fierce desire to capture Lord Warburton for Pansy and thus for himself, and consequently exhibits a new brutality towards Isabel in coldly urging her to promote the match, she being in a position to do so because Lord Warburton was once (is?) in love with her. He thus exhibits an unmasked vulgarity:

> 'You should have patience,' said Isabel. 'You know Englishmen are shy.'
> 'This one's not. He was not when he made love to *you*.'

And:

> 'You must have a great deal of influence with him,' Osmond went on at last. 'The moment you really wish it you can bring him to the point.' (Ch. XLI, p. 471)

At the same time he is assuming that, for motives worthy only of himself, she will hinder rather than help.

But even more important than this is an earlier scene, in Chapter XL, which occurs shortly after the return to their circle of Mme Merle. It is the first of a series in James's work where a character perceives something vital in an instant wordless look. It is an extreme refinement of the traditional 'catching red-handed' and is more important than that, because it generally includes a whole vision or intimation of a complex past, not just the simple present fact. It is a kind of shorthand for revelations which in life would take time to discover or guess at. Perhaps the most famous instance is in the late *The Wings of the Dove* (1902) where the heroine, Milly Theale, ignorant of any relation between her new friend Kate Croy and Merton Densher, with whom both girls are in love, realizes (amazingly) that he has returned to London simply from looking at Kate who in other ways is as usual:

Kate had positively but to be there just as she was to tell her he had come back It seemed to pass between them, in fine, without a word that he was in London, that he was perhaps only round the corner; and surely therefore no dealing of Milly's with her would yet have been so direct. (Ch. XIV)

This kind of thing thrills admirers of late James as much as it irritates readers who prefer something more straightforward. In any case Isabel's perception in *Portrait* is less arcane and is based on at least some evidence. Returning from a drive with Pansy in the Campagna she approaches the main rooms of the Palazzo. But:

Just beyond the threshold of the drawing-room she stopped short, the reason for her doing so being that she had received an impression. The impression had, in strictness, nothing unprecedented; but she felt it as something new, and the soundlessness of her step gave her time to take in the scene before she interrupted it. Madame Merle was there in her bonnet, and Gilbert Osmond was talking to her ... Madame Merle was standing on the rug, a little way from the fire; Osmond was in a deep chair, leaning back and looking at her ... her eyes were bent on his. What struck Isabel first was that he was sitting while Madame Merle stood; there was an anomaly in this that arrested her. Then she perceived that they had arrived at a desultory pause ... and were musing, face to face, with the freedom of old friends who sometimes exchange ideas without uttering them. There was nothing to shock in this; they were old friends in fact. But the thing made an image, lasting only a moment, like a sudden flicker of light. Their relative positions, their absorbed mutual gaze struck her as something detected. (pp. 457–8)

This 'sudden flicker of light' is, of course, to lead to the full glare of the Countess Gemini's exposure of the past in Chapter LI. For the moment, striking as it is, it serves brilliantly to prompt Isabel to probe further into where exactly she stands. And this she attempts, as we know, in Chapter XLII.

2. A Case for Osmond? (II)

As I have argued, the magnificent interior monologue which constitutes Chapter XLII is as much about Isabel's own confusion as it is about Osmond's character and the nature of their marriage. It is dramatic in that it reveals a developing series of ideas, interpretations, and new perceptions. It is not at all, as is often claimed, a definitive statement of a

static, objective truth. 'Suffering, with Isabel, was an active condition . . .
it was a passion of thought, of speculation, of response to every pressure.'
An important part of this process is that her initial and recurring indig-
nation, keyed off by Osmond's present behaviour, keeps on being qualified
by attempted mitigations of his past conduct. Thus 'It was, not her fault –
she had practised no deception; she had only admired and believed.'
(p. 474), becomes on the very next page '. . . if she had not deceived him
in intention she understood how completely she must have done so in fact.
She had effaced herself when he first knew her . . .' (p. 475) – and so on,
until 'it used to come over her . . . that she had deceived him at the very
first' (p. 482). Two striking things emerge from this train of thought.
First that James is evolving a brilliant variation on the traditional form
of deception, adultery: both parties have behaved, according to their
lights, entirely consistently and honourably. But since he has realized her
disdain of his 'traditions' ('hideously unclean') and his cynical contempt
for people, he is in a way right to feel that she is unfaithful to him and
not to be trusted. They are not compatible; both feel betrayed; both are
sincere; both are unhappy – and if this is so blame is irrelevant. But this
cannot be true – this sinless adultery – for Osmond remains – in spite of
the flaws Isabel both admits and unconsciously reveals in herself – an
extremely unpleasant man. The *impasse* thus created is profoundly
original to James (at least in English): actions do not here speak louder
than words, but thoughts louder than actions. This is a very forceful
kind of realism.

The second process initiated in the reader's mind by Isabel's pondering
is a close consideration of her husband's subsequent conduct. If while
condemning his character she has also seen justifications for him, even
when jarred by his recent callousness and her new suspicions, are we not
bound to follow her? If we accept the invitation to see what he does we
get closer to understanding the novel and better able to interpret its
strange ending. What then does he, saddled with so unsatisfactory a
situation, do? First of all, he becomes even more odious and intensifies
his arrogant yet covert self-seeking. We begin to be proficient in a language which might be called 'Osmondese', a language which has its own
horrible brilliance, and puts many more obvious literary villains in the
shade. It consists of a kind of relentless frigid bullying. This is a typical
exchange on the subject of Lord Warburton's possible proposal to
Pansy:

'What has become of Warburton? What does he mean by treating one like a
tradesman with a bill?'

'I know nothing about him,' Isabel said. '. . . He told me . . . that he meant to write to you.'

'He has never written to me.'

'So I supposed from your not having told me.'

'He's an odd fish,' said Osmond comprehensively. And on Isabel's making no rejoinder, he went on to enquire whether it took his lordship five days to indite a letter. 'Does he form his words with such precision?'

'I don't know,' Isabel was reduced to replying. 'I've never had a letter from him.'

'Never had a letter? I had an idea that you were at one time in intimate correspondence.' (Ch. XLVI, p. 521)

And so on. Everyone, I suppose, is capable of sarcasm, even if not so well phrased as this. But sarcasm is usually the result of anger and can be quickly softened by apology or even simple abstention. The point about Osmond's is that it is consistent, firm and coldly applied in furtherance of his aim. He appears never to occupy any middle ground between chilly politeness and overtly savage dismissal. A full demonstration of this could occupy pages. But any reader will remember the flavour of his exchanges with Isabel (and others). Perhaps the most lethal feature of his attack is its apparent calmness. Osmond would never shout, and this is what makes him so formidable an opponent. Yet he loads every word with malice and private anger and creates a rhetoric of venom which is all his own. A single long quotation is enough to illustrate his mastery:

'You're certainly not fortunate in your intimates; I wish you might make a new collection,' he said to her one morning . . . in a tone of ripe reflection which deprived the remark of all brutal abruptness. 'It's as if you had taken the trouble to pick out the people in the world that I have least in common with. Your cousin I've always thought a conceited ass – besides his being the most ill-favoured animal I know . . . His health seems to me the best part of him; it gives him privileges enjoyed by no one else. If he's so desperately ill there's only one way to prove it; but he seems to have no mind for that. I can't say much more for the great Warburton. When one really thinks of it, the cool insolence of that performance was something rare! He comes and looks at one's daughter as if she were a suite of apartments . . . Will you be so good as to draw up a lease? Then, on the whole, he decides that the rooms are too small; he doesn't think he could live on a third floor; he must look out for a *piano nobile* . . . Miss Stackpole, however, is your most wonderful invention. She strikes me as a kind of monster . . . Do you know what she reminds me of? Of a new steel pen – the most odious thing in nature. She talks as a steel pen writes; aren't her letters, by the way, on ruled paper? . . . I don't like at all to think she talks about me – I feel as I should feel if I knew the footman were wearing my hat.' (Ch. XLVII, pp. 537–8)

The insolent snobbish unfairness of this is devastating. Osmond is certainly a gifted man, for such cruel superciliousness can only be the product of a cultivated talent. But his virtuosity is not limited to attacks on Isabel. He can frighten the Countess Gemini with a hint (end of Ch. L, p. 579): and his patronage of Goodwood, whom he decides to like, is high comedy:

'There's a certain kind of vulgarity which I believe is really new ... Indeed I don't find vulgarity, at all, before the present century ... Now we've *liked you*! ... I'm talking for my wife as well as for myself, you see ... We're as united, you know, as the candlestick and the snuffers.' (Ch. XLVIII, p. 552)

And he rubs the 'we' in again and again. The comedy here is that Goodwood is so simple minded as not to notice the pinpricks so affably presented. As James says, perhaps superfluously:

Osmond knew very well what he was about, and that if he chose the tone of patronage with a grossness not in his habits he had an excellent reason for the escapade. Goodwood had only a vague sense that he was laying it on somehow ... he scarcely knew what Osmond was talking about; he wanted to be alone with Isabel ...(pp. 552–3)

So much, for the moment, for 'Osmondese'. The question that has to be answered is, roughly, 'Why does he behave like this?' If we step back for a moment it is clear that he has no real external grievances. He cannot, in any obvious sense, feel betrayed. He has gained a fortune and the actual loyalty of Isabel, however much he cares to misconstrue her. He can indulge to the fullest his wonderful taste for objets d'art. He occupies a palace in Rome. Although disappointed of Lord Warburton, he can expect many other candidates for Pansy's hand in marriage. Ralph is dying, and Goodwood fobbed off. He can control Mme Merle. And so on.

The most facile analysis of Osmond would, of course, be that his cool aggressiveness is the product of feelings of defensiveness. A natural reaction. But why should he have such feelings? The answer to this is revealed explicitly in Chapter XLIX, although the reader will probably in any case already have grasped it. He says to Mme Merle of Isabel:

'I asked very little; I only asked that she should like me.'

'That she should like you so much!'

'So much, of course; in such a case one asks the maximum. That she should adore me, if you will. Oh yes, I wanted that.'

'I never adored you,' said Madame Merle ...

'My wife has declined – declined to do anything of the sort,' said Osmond. 'If you're inclined to make a tragedy of that, the tragedy's hardly for her.'

'The tragedy's for me!' Madame Merle exclaimed ... (pp. 570–1)

Such a complex of tragedies – brought on by misunderstanding. We have to return, simply, to the fact that Osmond's grievance against Isabel is that she has an independent mind and being: that her 'ideas', however vaguely they are defined by her and for us, persist. When Osmond said in Chapter XXVI '*Dame* ... they must be sacrificed!', he was over-estimating his power. Here it is precisely that we return to the main point. Whatever we may think the relations between married persons should be – they certainly should not be this – all parties have acted in good faith as they then saw it. It is no good saying that Osmond, because of his vile verbal manifestations, is being arbitrarily nasty. He had genuine expectations, carefully stated, and these have been disappointed cruelly by Isabel's failure to 'adore' him. Good for her, one may well say, but also really unpleasant for him. A lesser man would have been content with formal submission and £70,000. But Osmond is an idealist: and his perversity is the product, however awful in itself, of disappointment and chagrin. In short he wishes to possess the internal and the external, and is denied the former while having been given good reason to expect it. In his own terms, he is perfectly genuine. And if we do not see it quite this way in the bustle of events – about Pansy, Warburton, Ralph, Goodwood, Henrietta, the Countess Gemini, Mme Merle – Isabel comes, in spite of it all and in the face of the Countess Gemini's sudden urgent and overflowing revelation of the hideous past, to recognize it.

The question is pushed to the extreme in the context of Ralph's last illness. Isabel's decision to go to England to see him is indeed determined emotionally by the Countess's conscientious warnings. But immediately before that, and in the same chapter (LI), Osmond has made his final and influential statement. It is important to realize how influential this is. On receipt of Mrs Touchett's telegram Isabel bursts in on him, interrupting a pointedly characteristic activity, the copying of a copy of an antique coin on to 'immaculate paper'. She is full of emotion and he of dry chill calm. So we expect, and at first get, the usual kind of scene between them:

'Excuse me for disturbing you,' she said.

'When I come into your room I always knock,' he answered, going on with his work.

'I forgot; I had something else to think of. My cousin's dying.'

'Ah, I don't believe that,' said Osmond, looking at his drawing through a magnifying glass. 'He was dying when we married; he'll outlive us all.' (p. 581)

There follows a passage of hateful hollow fencing in which Osmond's will to dominate becomes explicit: 'If you leave Rome to-day it will be a piece of the most deliberate, most calculated, opposition.' This forces her in turn to be, for the first time, explicit with him: 'I can't tell you how unjust you seem to me. But I think you know. It's your own opposition that's calculated. It's malignant.' But he refuses to be ruffled and expounds in full his consistent and – this is the trouble – genuine idea of their marriage and mutual obligations. It is a crisis for both of them, not just Isabel:

'I've never liked him [Ralph] and he has never liked me. That's why you like him – because he hates me,' said Osmond with a quick, barely audible tremor in his voice. (p. 583)

This is, of course, obviously perverse. But it is equally obviously what he, so perfectly ego-bound, really believes. He proceeds to expand on his dire philosophy of marriage:

'I take our marriage seriously; you appear to have found a way of not doing so. I'm not aware that we're divorced or separated; for me we are indissolubly united. You are nearer to me than any human creature, and I'm nearer to you. It may be a disagreeable proximity; it's one, at any rate, of our own deliberate making. You don't like to be reminded of that, I know; but I'm perfectly willing, because –' And he paused a moment, looking as if he had something to say which would be very much to the point. 'Because I think we should accept the consequences of our actions, and what I value most in life is the honour of a thing!'

He spoke gravely and almost gently; the accent of sarcasm had dropped out of his tone.

Isabel is literally baffled by this. (Even more cruelly baffled than Professor Geoffrey Moore who quotes these passages in his otherwise interesting introduction to the Penguin edition allows. She is 'caught in a mesh' which is both horrible, a total negation of even the most elementary individual freedom, and simultaneously contains a moral imperative which she cannot ignore:

His last words were not a command, they constituted a kind of appeal; and, though she felt that any expression of respect on his part could only be a refinement of egotism, they represented something transcendent and absolute, like the sign of the cross or the flag of one's country. He spoke in the name of something sacred and precious – the observance of a magnificent form.

This is a vital recognition of value on Isabel's part, so it is important that we should be clear about it. The most deceptive words for students of literature are not the ones which have dropped out of use ('bodkin' for dagger, or 'bourn' for region or country, for example) but those which are still current but have altered their meaning. In the eighteenth century 'facetious' meant something like lively, sociable and witty; now it means silly or superficially humorous. The same is true of institutions. If we were to read about a trial by combat in which the winner (directed by Providence) was shown to be *right* and not just better at fighting or lucky, then we would know that an archaic custom was being described. In the present case the central issue, marital obligation, is still with us, as are the metaphors drawn from Christianity and patriotism.But because these things are more loosely considered, less imperative, than they were a hundred years ago, the contemporary reader may feel Osmond's appeal to be 'dated in a way that damages the book, or even, to the superficial, quaint. Which is one reason why there is so much debate about the ending. We have therefore to be quite clear as to what is essentially at stake: and this is contained in the view, not limited to its particular context, that 'we should accept the consequences of our actions'. It is a powerful argument which even an anarchist might have trouble in dismissing. 'Untune that string,/And hark what discord follows', as Shakespeare's Ulysses says of a different matter in *Troilus and Cressida*. The point is formidable in spite of the character who makes it. Which is perhaps why James has to resort to Osmond's melodramatically villainous past in order for Isabel, temporarily at least, to find any way forward at all. She can depart after her conversation with the Countess Gemini, but in confusion rather than in peace. Osmond's argument is bound to remain in her mind, to trouble her, whatever she now does. And we should note in passing that the other 'villain', the accomplished Mme Merle, quite humbly accepts the consequences of *her* past – as we soon see.

3. Towards the End

The story is now prepared for, and hastening toward, its end. But before discussing this, it is necessary to consider where the other characters are left, and, in turn, what the nature of their influence might be.

Pansy has priority because it is to her that Isabel must go before her departure. The result is dispiriting. In Chapter L, immediately before the crisis with Osmond, Isabel has been witness to an extremely touching scene in the Coliseum (that decayed, bloody and unhealthy relic of savage power in which James's Daisy Miller had previously confronted her fate). The *diminuendo* lovers, Pansy and Rosier, suddenly expand or mutely explode into a surprisingly lavish emotion. Rosier has sacrificed almost all his cherished bibelots for Pansy and feels 'half a head taller in consequence'; this would be entirely comic were we not led to see that it is a real sacrifice and the exact opposite of what his fellow connoisseur, Osmond, had done or would be capable of doing. 'I had done all that I could, and no Man is well pleased to have his all neglected, be it ever so little,' as Dr Johnson gloomily remarked in his famous letter of rebuke to Lord Chesterfield. And Pansy reciprocates in her distinctive way: about to leave with Isabel she 'at first kept her eyes fixed on her lap: then she raised them':

> There shone out of each of them a little melancholy ray – a spark of timid passion which touched Isabel to the heart. At the same time a wave of envy passed over her soul, as she compared the tremulous longing, the definite ideal of the child with her own dry despair. 'Poor little Pansy!' she affectionately said.
> 'Oh, never mind!' Pansy answered in a tone of eager apology. (p. 575)

The use of adjectives such as 'little', 'timid', 'tremulous' should not mislead us into thinking of this as pathetic or 'sentimental' in a self-indulgent way. Or, if it does superficially resemble the weaker parts of Victorian fiction, then the reader is brusquely reawakened by Osmond's immediate sentence of his daughter to comfortable imprisonment in the Convent.

To the Convent therefore Isabel must go. And here she, herself, desperate, encounters only examples of defeat and oppression. Mme Merle is there and quietly abdicates her position as manipulator of appearances:

> 'You don't see why I should have come; it's as if I had anticipated you. I confess I've been rather indiscreet – I ought to have asked your permission.' There was none of the oblique movement of irony in this; it was said simply and mildly ... (Ch. LII, p. 596)

She attempts to keep up her front – 'but there were phrases and gradations in her speech ... She had not proceeded far before Isabel noted a sudden break in her voice, a lapse in her continuity, which was in itself a complete drama ...' The drama consists, of course, in Mme Merle's implicit apology for being Pansy's mother, an unacknowledged mother disliked by her daughter, rejected by the father, and at the end of her great resources. Isabel restrains, to her credit, what could have been a natural outbreak of rage:

> What remained was the cleverest woman in the world standing there within a few feet of her and knowing as little what to think as the meanest. Isabel's only revenge was to be silent still – to leave Mme Merle in this unprecedented situation. (p. 598)

More depression follows. Pansy too is broken:

'. . . I've thought a great deal.'

'What have you thought?'

'Well, that I must never displease papa.'

'You knew that before.'

'Yes; but I know it better. I'll do anything – I'll do anything,' said Pansy. Then, as she heard her own words, a deep, pure blush came into her face. Isabel read the meaning of it; she saw the poor girl had been vanquished. It was as well that Mr Edward Rosier had kept his enamels! (p. 602)

Such accumulating pathos can serve only to lay a further obligation on Isabel: ' "I won't desert you," she said at last.' This is bad enough. Poor Isabel, again. But James is quite relentless. It is now that he has Mme Merle reveal to Isabel the ultimate nastiness of the situation, to unleash on her the pivotal irony underlying the action: 'it was your uncle's money, but it was your cousin's idea . . . Ah, my dear, the sum was large!' With that the chastened manipulator, like Dick Diver in F. Scott Fitzgerald's *Tender is the Night*, evaporates into a banefully neutral plane of existence. 'I shall go to America,' Mme Merle says: and this reminds one in secular terms of the bitter lament of the shade of Achilles in Book XI of the *Odyssey*: 'Better I say, to break sod as a farm hand/for some poor countryman, on iron rations, than lord it over all the exhausted dead' (Robert Fitzgerald's translation).

This point is the nadir of the book. Almost everybody, including Osmond, has been defeated, disappointed or dismissed. But such a series of depressing failures and complicated confinements demands a release at the same time as suggesting a conclusion. What is Isabel, betrayed and self-betrayed, cut off from imagination and freedom, to do? Suspense, that necessary quality, is heightened. How can it be resolved? First of all, and temporarily, by a reintroduction of the comic note in a further account of Henrietta and Mr Bantling, which is so clear as to need no commentary. Second, and crucially, by the scene of Ralph's death and the recognition of value which this involves. Isabel has been used, manipulated, or, as she delicately puts it to Mrs Touchett, 'made a convenience of' by Mme Merle and Osmond. This, for James, is the worst thing, morally speaking, that a person can have done to them – the very negation of freedom and choice. Now she confronts the benevolent but mistaken cause. No wonder that they behave like children, for like children they have trusted a world that cannot be trusted. James wrote a fine essay on *The Tempest* in 1907; but it is another late play of Shakespeare, *The Winter's Tale*, that comes to mind:

We were as twinn'd lambs that did frisk i' th'sun,
And bleat the one at th'other: what we chang'd

Was innocence for innocence: we knew not
The doctrine of ill-doing, nor dream'd
That any did . . . (Act I, Scene 2)

says King Polixenes. It is in a mood resembling this that Ralph and Isabel finally meet in a version of the death scene so often met with in Victorian novels. One of the conditions of this mode is that one party at least should be radically innocent or have become totally repentant. Death is a clearing of the slate both literally and morally. It would be hard to argue that this is not true to life. But James's version is, as we might expect, complicated. Both actors are innocent in intention, but in act half guilty. So we have the traditional manner of sentiment first:

'You've been like an angel beside my bed. You know they talk about the angel of death. It's the most beautiful of all. You've been like that; as if you were waiting for me.'
'I was not waiting for your death; I was waiting for – for this. This is not death, dear Ralph.'
'Not for you – no. There's nothing that makes us feel so much alive as to see others die. That's the sensation of life – the sense that we remain.' (Ch. LIV, p. 620)

Isabel however (though she may be claimed by symbol-hunters as Artemis/Diana – the Archer) is no Valkyrie, and Ralph no Siegmund. The situation remains extremely human and therefore compromised:

'Is it true – is it true?' she asked.
'True that you've been stupid? Oh no,' said Ralph with a sensible intention of wit.
'That you made me rich – that all I have is yours?'
He turned away his head, and for some time said nothing. Then at last: 'Ah, don't speak of that – that was not happy.' Slowly he moved his face towards her again, and they once more saw each other. 'But for that – but for that –!' And he paused. 'I believe I ruined you,' he wailed. (p. 621)

And this, at Ralph's last hour, becomes a subject of discussion. Isabel has the idea 'that they were looking at the truth together' – and she says of Osmond that 'He married me for the money' – that dire recognition from which she has not yet recovered – but Ralph superbly answers back with a truth which, as I have argued, is essential: 'He was greatly in love with you.' But again qualifies this with:

'You wanted to look at life for yourself – but you were not allowed; you were punished for your wish. You were ground in the very mill of the conventional!' (p. 622)

66

This death-bed, considering and balancing to the last, is far from ordinary. Therefore the value it asserts, although if it were not in this context it might sound a banal catch-all, gains a certain potency. 'But love remains,' says Ralph. This assertion, far from being comforting, becomes part of the final challenge for Isabel. What content can 'love' for her now have?

4. The End

Isabel is cut off from all the likely sources of love, or even comfort. Mrs Touchett has drily recognized, in the death of her son, a final break with properly sentient being. A fate which curiously links her with Osmond, minus his active malignancy:

... it had come over her dimly that she had failed of something, that she saw herself in the future as an old woman without memories. Her little sharp face looked tragical. (Ch. LIV, p. 616)

She cannot help Isabel, save as a warning. Warburton too is to be married (good for him) and is thus unavailable in any capacity: 'She had known him only as a suitor, and now that was all over. He was dead for poor Pansy; by Pansy he might have lived' (p. 618). We note that Isabel's imagination is still alive, but the chance has gone.

The plain fact is that everyone important, with three exceptions, is either literally or metaphorically dead. The exceptions are Osmond, Pansy and Caspar Goodwood. The latter must be, for the moment, the most important. Just before her trip to the Middle East, newly endowed with her fortune, gently wooed by Osmond, Isabel had felt that 'The world lay before her – she could do whatever she chose' (Ch. XXXI, p. 373). Although, as I have remarked, James is little given to literary references, this one could escape none but the most illiterate. David Galloway (see reading list) has already remarked on part of it. Dickens himself had used it at the end of *Great Expectations*. The reference is to the close of *Paradise Lost* – some of the most famous lines in English – when Adam and Eve descend from the Eden of innocence to the world of the real and of sin suffering:

> Some natural tears they drop'd, but wip'd them soon;
> The World was all before them, where to choose
> Their place of rest, and Providence their guide:
> They hand in hand with wand'ring steps and slow,
> Through *Eden* took their solitary way.

Milton's emphasis is on 'hand in hand' and so is that of Dickens: 'I took her hand in mine, and we went out . . .' Isabel's is on *herself*. So it is entirely appropriate that Goodwood should appear, pressing her to marry him, in the next chapter. No good, as we know. But at least he is relentlessly active as an alternative. He remains so intermittently. When he reappears in Rome in Chapter XLVII, he seems to Isabel a nuisance, a disagreeable reminder of unpleasant challenges in the past:

He had come to her with his unhappiness when her own bliss was so perfect; he had done his best to darken the brightness of those pure rays. He had not been violent, and yet there had been a violence in the impression. There had been a violence at any rate in something somewhere . . . (p. 533)

And so on. Now that her happiness has departed he must be an even less welcome appearance in his 'bareness and bleakness' and his ability to suggest violence 'in something somewhere' – quite possibly in Isabel herself and especially in the context of her passionless and hopeless marriage. On this occasion, after another blunt declaration of love, he departs on the heels of Lord Warburton and with the dying Ralph. And now, in Chapter LV, with Ralph dead, the soon to be married Warburton just having taken his leave, he comes back for the last time with characteristic or even enhanced abruptness. Isabel has no defence or buffer. She is morally free from Osmond – and could presumably become legally so. In previous encounters she has always had the defence of not wanting to marry, or wanting to marry someone else, or being married. Or, at least, that is the view that Goodwood can legitimately take. The miserable Isabel is at her most vulnerable to his overtly masculine attack. It is therefore entirely appropriate that her first words upon his seizing her wrist on the historic bench at Gardencourt are 'You've frightened me' (p. 631). She had every reason to be frightened. Most of the (extensive) critical commentary on the ensuing scene concentrates on the clearly sexual nature of the action – his kiss – and the violent metaphors James uses to describe it:

. . . she had never been loved before. She had believed it, but this was different; this was the hot wind of the desert, at the approach of which the others dropped dead, like mere sweet airs of the garden. It wrapped her about; it lifted her off her feet, while the very taste of it, as of something potent, acrid and strange, forced open her set teeth. (p. 634)

And crucially:

His kiss was like white lightning, a flash that spread, and spread again, and stayed; and it was extraordinarily as if, while she took it, she felt each thing in his hard manhood that had least pleased her, each aggressive fact of his face, his figure, his presence, justified of its intense identity and made one with this act of possession. So had she heard of those wrecked and under water following a train of images before they sink. But when darkness returned, she was free. (pp. 635–6)

This is, at least, clear in general import. What is commonly objected is that the melodrama of deserts, lightning, wrecks and drowning sorts badly with the urbanity of style we are used to; a polite way of saying that James was not good at rendering the obviously physical, and jars the reader when he attempts it. I would prefer to say that it is both necessary and bold for him to try, and that the point is emphatically made. James was not D. H. Lawrence, but nor was Lawrence James. Isabel needs to encounter sexual fright in the completion of her experience, concretely as well as theoretically (we forget that oddly arbitrary baby), and here it is: 'this was different'.

But because of the prominence of this issue what is really radical in the scene can be (is) too easily overlooked. Goodwood is proposing a break with the 'ghastly form', her marriage, as well as kissing her. The content of his argument might be called something like 'existential', and it has a powerful logic which is the deliberately complete opposite of the codes so malignly espoused by Osmond but *also* more or less agreed to by everyone else in the book, and, I suppose, the reader while reading. He is able to attack not only the hollow forms of Osmond and Mme Merle but also the assumed and pleasant certainties of the nice people in the book. He proposes 'freedom' in a mode which is very remote indeed from Isabel's or Ralph's previous toyings with it. Indeed he is spurred to a kind of gritty eloquence which it is hard for us, as well as for Isabel, to resist:

Why shouldn't we be happy . . .? Here I stand; I'm as firm as a rock. What have you to care about? You've no children; that perhaps would be an obstacle. As it is, you've nothing to consider. You must save what you can of your life . . . It would be an insult to you to assume that you care for the look of the thing, for what people say, for the bottomless idiocy of the world. We've nothing to do with all that; we're quite out of it; we look at things as they are. (p. 634)

Well, yes – but it may be objected that the happiness proposed in 'why shouldn't we be happy?' is based on an assumption of irresponsible superiority – of an elevation above 'what people say' in their 'bottomless idiocy'. If Mr Goodwood is 'as firm as a rock' it is because he is not only a forceful man, but also a rich one. No pauper could be so confident. And presumably the idiots have bought his cotton goods. He also assumes, of course, that his 'we' automatically includes Isabel. Why should it? – and why should he bind her to his own version of 'form'? He has had no encouragement to believe that he is for Isabel much more than a harassing bore. Yet he is too acute to have missed these points. He supplies more arguments:

> You took the great step in coming away; the next is nothing; it's the natural one. I swear, as I stand here, that a woman deliberately made to suffer is justified in anything in life – in going down into the streets if that will help her! I know how you suffer, and that's why I'm here. We can do absolutely as we please; to whom under the sun do we owe anything? What is it that holds us, what is it that has the smallest right to interfere in such a question as this? Such a question is between ourselves – and to say that is to settle it! Were we born to rot in our misery – were we born to be afraid? . . . The world's all before us . . . (pp. 634–5)

Artful echoes of Milton's fall again – from 'The world lay before her' we have come much closer to 'The world was all before them' in his 'The world's all before us'. But is it? The appeals in this speech are to the 'natural' (a dubious concept); to comparison with all ill-treated women (compassionate but is it relevant?), and again to the rhetoric of a new life, a decisive hope. 'Were we born to rot . . .?' Obviously not, especially when reinforced by a decisive kiss. The reader may well want Isabel to succumb. But while we do not know how much she is attracted to Goodwood and his first-rate persuasions, we sympathize with her flight. Goodwood, after all, has given his case away in asking 'to whom under the sun do we owe anything . . .' – and his case for hope might be answered by the relevant stress in the first stanza of Dr Johnson's 'Ode on the Death of Dr Robert Levet' (1783):

> Condemn'd to hopes delusive mine.
> As on we toil from day to day,
> By sudden blasts, or slow decline,
> Our social comforts drop away.

What 'social comforts' – the support, company, sanction and sharing of a common civilization – can Goodwood by his own sheer force supply? This is the acute question posed by the end of *Portrait*. And the answer, although meagre, can be satisfying.

Osmond's appeal to the importance of accepting the results of one's actions may be dry to the point of suffocation; but it is still powerful. Also its force for Isabel is implicit in a great deal of what has gone before. Oddly – or is it? – Isabel's free spirit, so much advertised at the start of the book, is, by the end, more naturally attuned to a dreary and unglamorous fulfilment of obligation than it is to the assertive cutting off of all other ties in favour of the self-sufficient 'we' which Goodwood proposes. Isabel has to get away in order to imprison herself. A grim paradox of course, but more credible than floating off to the happiness (*that* dubious concept) of life purely *à deux* with a lover with whom we doubt she is really in love. Clint Eastwood remarks in *Magnum Force* (1973) that a person has to know his own limitations. Trite but true. It is a truth that Isabel now faces. Why is she able to face it?

The answer to this question is so obvious as to have eluded critics who have not noticed the clues, extremely carefully planted, that James has already given us about Isabel's general attitude. She is, morally, an idealist: and it is part of her plight that Osmond's challenge to her in Chapter LI strikes a previously existent chord. She is more than ripe for his attack. In Chapter XLV for instance, she reflects in the context of Osmond's disapproval of her visiting Ralph in Rome:

It was not that she loved Ralph less, but that almost anything seemed preferable to repudiating the most serious act – the single sacred act – of her life ... To break with Osmond once would be to break for ever; any open acknowledgement of their irreconcilable needs would be an admission that their whole attempt had proved a failure ... They had attempted only one thing, but that one thing was to have been exquisite. Once they missed it nothing else would do; there was no conceivable substitute for that success ... the measure of propriety was in the canon of taste, and there couldn't have been a better proof that morality was, so to speak, a matter of earnest application. (p. 511)

'So to speak' is here really a matter of speaking to oneself – intimately. And unfortunately, there is no chance that Isabel will be able to catch with Osmond's surcease success. He shows no sign of dying. Nevertheless Isabel's word is her bond in a manner so emphatic as to guarantee to the attentive reader Goodwood's failure. Henrietta is, of course, Goodwood's sponsor. But in conversation with her and again before Osmond's ultimatum, we learn from the now candid Isabel that:

'I don't know what great unhappiness may bring me to; but it seems to me that I shall always be ashamed. One must accept one's deeds. I married him before all the world; I was perfectly free; it was impossible to do anything more deliberate. One can't change that way,' Isabel repeated.

'You *have* changed, in spite of the impossibility ... Don't you think you're rather too considerate?'

'It's not of him that I'm considerate – it's of myself,' Isabel answered. (Ch. XLVII, p. 536)

Nothing could be plainer. Nothing could be more evasive. It is a version of the Soldier's Oath: in deliberately and publicly swearing obedience, ('the single sacred act') to something or someone a person is at once binding and freeing themselves. Thus so long as one does not break faith

71

with the oath, one can feel justified in acting towards others as seems appropriate or expedient: yet with regard to the subject of the oath all freedom is lost. A drastic example of this morality may be found in the often asserted explanation of the failure of the German Army in the Second World War to dispose of the maniac Hitler. His policies threatened not only the welfare of that unsurpassed killing machine, and of their country, but also themselves. They felt perfectly at liberty to kill anyone else, which they did with excellent efficiency: but also as perfectly bound not to kill *him*. This is, of course, an example of moral absolutism carried to an absurd and even pitiable length – an old European tradition. But it is in the context of the merely domestic that Isabel is charged with – or contaminated by – the same ethic. 'It's not of him that I'm considerate – it's of myself': in the subfusc light cast by this remark it should be no surprise at all that Isabel will not, cannot and could never accept Goodwood's version of freedom, even if she wanted to, which one doubts.

Portrait, however, is not a blunt moral treatise. Towards Rome must Isabel go. 'There was a very straight path.' All roads lead to Rome, as we know; but strait paths also lead to virtue. Isabel has promised Osmond in public. But in private she has also promised Pansy. If we look for alleviation from the general grimness of the ending, it is to be in the image of that sweetly wistful young person. She represents a possible future which her step-mother for herself, so initially free, has abnegated. Henrietta has been typically dismissive while raising, equally typically, the point:

> 'Well ... I've only one criticism to make. I don't see why you promised little Miss Osmond to go back.'
> 'I'm not sure I see myself now,' Isabel replied. 'But I did it then.'
> 'If you've forgotten your reason perhaps you won't return.'
> Isabel waited a moment. 'Then perhaps I shall find another.'
> 'You'll certainly never find a good one.'
> 'In default of a better my having promised will do,' Isabel suggested. (Ch. LIII, p. 611)

Of course it would be idle to speculate on how much Isabel will be able to do for Pansy or even how she will be received by Osmond. But there is at least a glimmer of hope – which there is not for Goodwood, as James's revision of his final paragraph makes clear.

If not a tragic it is nonetheless certainly not a happy ending. The satisfaction that the reader feels is, I suppose, less dependent on external events than on the sense that the portrait has been finished. Isabel has run her course, has changed, or been changed, by the exercise of her beloved freedom, and turned from a lively *ingénue* from the New World into a rather reserved lady devoted mainly to an austere sense of duty and obligation. But she has survived and manifests a wholly convincing dignity and integrity. This, James must have felt, was enough for the modern novel of which he was the leading exponent in English. It is not an 'open-ended' work of the kind favoured by some of our contemporaries: we know very well what has happened and there is no 'ambiguity'. But even more emphatically, it is not the kind of work which many of his contemporaries would have liked the 'pessimistic' Mr James to write. It lacks, as he puts it charmingly in his essay 'The Art of Fiction' (1884):

. . . a 'happy ending' . . . a distribution at the last of prizes, pensions, husbands, wives, babies, millions, appended paragraphs and cheerful remarks.

Many people still like this kind of ending. I do. But James is pursuing and achieving a new realism, with marvellous intelligence and magnificent results. 'To judge wrong, I think, is more honourable than not to judge at all,' Isabel spiritedly remarks to Goodwood early on (Ch. XVI, p. 214). She has done this and taken on the consequences, however painful and costly. And her good faith has injured no one, with the possible exception of Osmond. It is hard to see what more could be needed.

5. Conclusion

The present study has gone over a good deal of the familiar ground covered by commentators, sometimes ploddingly, on *Portrait*. It has also raised a few fresh points. But in this process something has been missed out, namely: wit. In considering 'one of the two most brilliant novels in the language' I have left it to the reader to register the comedy which accompanies so many of the developments and which accounts for an abundance of epigrams conveying truth, generated by James's extraordinarily urbane manner. Henrietta is a constant source of comedy, of course. The Countess Gemini as well. There is also a spate of remarks which both lighten and enforce the point. For example – one out of many – it is hard to imagine a reader who would not get a kind of pleasure, as well as an influential truth, out of the reason for Osmond's insistence on Isabel keeping up her 'Thursday evenings' in Rome: '. . . to which her husband still held for the sake not so much of inviting people as of not inviting them'. (Ch. XLVII, p. 541). A laugh of course, but also a shudder. No wonder that James resented Oscar Wilde's success – while compassionating at his subsequent downfall. At any rate, a joke is a joke – and that is all that can be said about it. You 'get' it or you do not: no amount of commentary can make it funny or purposeful if it is not grasped with ease. Therefore I have assumed that readers will be able to be amused without superfluous comment.

Such readers will at least admit the justice of the plea that a prime requirement is that the author must have: '. . . the benefit, whatever it may be, involved in his having cast a spell upon the simpler, the very simplest, forms of attention. That is all he's entitled to.' (1908 Preface). We should read *Portrait* in this light: and then go on to the 'finer tribute' of the reader's 'reflection or discrimination'. Any sensible person will reflect and discriminate without compulsion. It is the happy task of that maligned busybody, the commentator, to assist in the process.

Appendix: a Note on the Texts

The Portrait of a Lady was subjected by James to a number of minor revisions. The most important of these was for the 'Collective' Edition of 1883 (Macmillan). This pales, however, beside the extensive refurbishing carried out for the *New York Edition* (1907–9) by the older James, who had by then developed what he considered his definitive style. This is the version to which I have been referring.

Opinions vary as to the character and excellence of the various texts. A powerful consensus prefers the *New York Edition*, which is why it is now most often printed (for example, by Penguin Books). I prefer the earlier versions.

The general difference, very generally stated, is that the older James injected an added subtlety and precision in *nuance* and metaphor. This is of course a gain. But in the process he had to let go a certain brisk, fresh, forthright crispness.

Those interested in this question should consult (among others):

(a) F. O. Matthiessen, *Henry James: the Major Phase,* New York, 1944; reprinted 1963 – in his appendix 'The Painter's Sponge and Varnish Bottle'; and (b) Sidney J. Krause, *American Literature*, XXX, March 1958, 76–88.

For those not interested in the various editions, it should be emphasized that it is only the phraseology that is altered; the story, characters and so on remain the same.

Selected Reading

1. Primary

1. Most of *James's Fiction* is currently available in paperbacks: some other works will have to be sought in libraries. Concentrate first on the fiction.

2. James's *Literary Criticism*: the most extensive selection is in 'The Library of America' series, selected and edited by Leon Edel and Mark Wilson, in two volumes (New York, 1984; Cambridge, 1984).

3. James's *Letters*: the largest collection so far is edited by Leon Edel, in four volumes (Cambridge [Mass.]; London, 1974–84). There are only a few trivial errors in this edition.

4. James's *Notebooks*: F. O. Matthiessen and Kenneth B. Murdock (eds) (New York, 1955).

5. James's *Autobiography*: F. W. Dupee (ed.) (London, 1956). This is a reprint of three (incomplete) volumes published by James in 1913, 1914 and (posthumously) 1917.

2. Secondary

(a) Life, etc.:

1. Leon Edel, *The Life of Henry James*. This was originally published in five volumes from 1953 to 1972. It is now most readily available as a 'Definitive Edition' (Harmondsworth, 1977) and contains a vast amount of information.

2. Roger Gard (ed.), *Henry James: the Critical Heritage*, London, 1968. This is a collection of opinions; those of James's contemporaries of him and his of them.

3. Norman Page (ed.), *Henry James: Interviews and Recollections*, London, 1968. An illuminating series of anecdotes.

(b) Criticism:

This is an intimidatingly huge field. The following is, therefore, only a minute sample of what might be found useful and *excludes what has already been mentioned* in the text.

1. Marius Bewley, *The Eccentric Design: Form in the Classic American Novel* (London, 1959).

2. Davıa Galloway, *The Portrait of a Lady* (London, 1967).

3. F. R. Leavis, *The Great Tradition* (London, 1948). Contains two seminal chapters on James.

4. Richard Poirier, *The Comic Sense of Henry James*, London, 1960.

5. Philip Rahv, *Image and Idea* (Norfolk, Conn., 1957). Contains a nicely individual view.

6. William T. Stafford (ed.), *Perspectives on James's 'The Portrait of a Lady'* (London and New York, 1967). A valuable collection of essays up to 1967.

MORE ABOUT PENGUINS, PELICANS, PEREGRINES AND PUFFINS

For further information about books available from Penguins please write to Dept EP, Penguin Books Ltd, Harmondsworth, Middlesex UB8 0DA.

In the U.S.A.: For a complete list of books available from Penguins in the United States write to Dept DG, Penguin Books, 299 Murray Hill Parkway, East Rutherford, New Jersey 07073.

In Canada: For a complete list of books available from Penguins in Canada write to Penguin Books Canada Ltd, 2801 John Street, Markham, Ontario L3R 1B4.

In Australia: For a complete list of books available from Penguins in Australia write to the Marketing Department, Penguin Books Australia Ltd, P.O. Box 257, Ringwood, Victoria 3134.

In New Zealand: For a complete list of books available from Penguins in New Zealand write to the Marketing Department, Penguin Books (N.Z.) Ltd, Private Bag, Takapuna, Auckland 9.

In India: For a complete list of books available from Penguins in India write to Penguin Overseas Ltd, 706 Eros Apartments, 56 Nehru Place, New Delhi 110019.